This anthology features winning entries from an annual competition which is free to enter. Winners also receive a free copy of the anthology. If you would like to enter for next year's anthology, send a loose second class stamp and three poems, each of 20 lines and 160 words maximum, to United Press, 1 Yorke Street, Burnley, BB11 1HD by the annual closing date of July 31st.
You can also call us on 01282 459533 or visit our website on upltd.co.uk

Cover photo of the River Dee at Chester by courtesy of The North West Tourist Board.

Published in Great Britain by
United Press Limited.
2000
ISBN 1-902803-21-3
© Contributors
All Rights Reserved

www.upltd.co.uk

National Poetry Anthology 2000

Foreword

One literary expert said recently - "Every great writer gets recognised eventually. No exceptional talent goes undiscovered for long." I couldn't disagree more. Thousands of great writers are rejected every day. Thousand of abysmal books roll off the presses every hour. This is because modern literature is governed by parasites. Their main concern is ordering another Chardonnay on their expense account. Their main motivation is getting a company car with an LSi instead of an LS. These people are in control of our literary heritage. They gain promotion by discovering writers who sell books, not writers who produce literature. The test of a good manuscript is now - "How many people will buy it?" not - "How good is it?"

I am delighted to say that the National Poetry Anthology has no such restrictions. We search for the best. And most of these winners have the delight of seeing themselves in print for the first time. If the cocktail wallahs who run publishing houses had their way these writers would never see the light of day. That is why I am so delighted to be associated with the NPA. It is a breath of fresh air in an art which has become an industry, where words like talent and genius are replaced by profit and loss. Personally I think it is time to throw the moneylenders out of the temple and let this particular art form open itself to the real artists - our new breed of talented writers.

Peter Quinn, Editor.

Contents

Each poet listed in this contents of the 2000 National Poetry Anthology is a winner in his or her own right. Their poems were selected as winners for their town or area in a free-to-enter annual competition which featured many thousands of entries. The winners are grouped into various regions. If you do not find a winner from your locality this is because insufficient entries were received from that area.

SOUTH EAST - Pages 9 - 38
John Harper-Smith, High Wycombe, Ellen Potter, Milton Keynes, Louise Ryder, Amersham, Neil Innes, Buckingham, Valerie Harvey, Chesham, Sarah Brown, Aldershot, Phil Heath, Letchworth, Alexandra Singleton, Welwyn Garden City, Joyce Walker, Borehamwood, Kevin Moylett, Southampton, Lisa Chandler, Basingstoke, Mark Smith, Bordon, Audrey Cameron-Cowburn, Gosport, Lucy Vaughan, Alton, Brian Dennis, Biggleswade, Dolly Harmer, Leighton Buzzard, Dennis Mabey, Bedford, Pat House, Thatcham, Pamela Gardener, Maidenhead, Carol Sutherland, Windsor, Amanda Sanderson, Newbury, Judith MacBeth, Reading, Keith Strangwood, Banbury, T Robertson, Abingdon, Jim Sargant, Thame, Kenneth Webb, Bicester, Dympna Pyle, Henley-on-Thames, Jean Gray, Eastbourne, Claire Shelton-Jones, Brighton, Neil Dickson, Hove, Kay Green, Hastings, Sally Selmes, St Leonards-on-Sea, Carole Blacher, Orpington, Christine Finnis, Maidstone, Diane Watson, Dover, Nola Small, Bromley, Cye Thomas, Chatham, Joan Todd, Chislehurst, Chris Lee-Rowden, Whitstable, Tanya Stephens, Dartford, Eleanor Marshall, Gillingham, Gavin Rodney, Uxbridge, Peter Burns, Ealing, Nicola York, Wimbledon, Mary Baird-Hammond, Chelsea, Joy Lennick, Romford, Verity Burgess, Chelmsford, V Foulger, Canvey Island, Betty Davis, Southend, Jean Owen, Westcliff, Beverley Cope, Wallington, Kate Crowther, Godalming, Juliette Seel, Morden, Dr Andrew Cunningham, Guildford, Barry Tebb, Sutton.

SOUTH WEST - Pages 39 - 54
Jane Eagle, Radstock, Peter Lewis, Bath, Andrew Nash, Bristol, Chris Bond, Exeter, Peter Atha, Paignton, Victoria Ewan, Torquay, Tony Cloke, Okehampton, Martin Wildman, Newton Abbot, A Bradbury, Salisbury, Simon Russell, Swindon, Jerry Toman, Camborne, Barney Hill, Redruth, Josie Hodges, Bodmin, Janine Vallor, Bridport, Dorothy Davis-Sellick, Poole, Elsie Torrent, Bournemouth, Marj Phelpstead, Gloucester, Susan Amos, Cinderford, Michael Henry, Cheltenham, Tom Sage, Frome, Belinda Harris, Chard, Alison Ashby, Yeovil, Paul Tipney, Bridgwater, Lynda Dickson, Taunton.

WALES - Pages 55 - 61
Kay Willding, Pontypridd, Geraldine Parr, Chepstow, Derek Morgan, Aberdare, Maggie Bevan, Colwyn Bay, Samantha Crofts, Cardiff, Patricia Newton, Caerphilly, Rebecca Rees, Ammanford, Neil Cunningham, Tenby, Helen Miles, Bridgend.

WEST MIDLANDS - Pages 62 - 75
Leslie Grice, Burton-on-Trent, Annette Jones, Cannock, Bobbie Dee, Leamington Spa, Dorothy Thompson, Stratford, Sue Minton, Rugby, Spencer Winnett, Stourport-on-Severn, Robert Collins, Hereford, Patrick Rooke, Evesham, Ann Weavers, Kidderminster, Matthew Thomas, Ludlow, Isobel Stone, Shrewsbury,

Craig Welburn, Whitchurch, John Cooper, Stourbridge, Jo Gaskin, Solihull, Kerry Lewis, Wolverhampton, Alice Smith, Birmingham, Marie Evans, Coventry, Matt Nunn, Sutton Coldfield, Anthony Mace, Stoke, Akkeber Osborne, Telford.

EAST MIDLANDS - Pages 76 - 88
Graham Smith, Kettering, Martin Heseltine, Lincoln, Linda Moore, Scunthorpe, Louise Law, Louth, Gary Wright, Gainsborough, Betty Clark, Skegness, James Smith, Chesterfield, Sheila Sharpe, Derby, Anne Shimwell, Bakewell, Patricia Wells, Matlock, Daniel Morley, Ripley, Margaret Jackson, Swadlincote, Heather-Julie Hollingsworth, Coalville, Priya Chauhan, Loughborough, Kaye Axon, Leicester, Teresa Shelton, Retford, Vikki Styles, Nottingham, Dominic Allard, Northampton, Elizabeth Morton, Wellingborough, Edward Mitchell, Corby.

EAST ANGLIA - Pages 89 - 96
Campanula Downes, Bury St Edmunds, Sarah Stone, Cromer, Donald Watts, King's Lynn, K Lake, Gt Yarmouth, Patricia Rudduck, Parson Drove, Louis Barrow, March, Diana Moules, Wisbech, Rosemary Westwell, Ely, Ann Bennett, Haverhill, Val McCurdy, Lowestoft, Janet Cross, Peterborough, Norman Mitchell, Downham Market.

NORTH WEST - Pages 97 - 106
Beryl Newcombe, Liverpool, Thomas Graham, Barrow, Bertha Bishop, Lancaster, Doris Hester, Blackpool, David Edwards, Ormskirk, John Bryant, Burnley, Hilda Naughton, Colne, Sheila Farrer, Heywood, Steve Buttrick, Wilmslow, Peter Goldberg, Manchester, Pauline Barker, Bolton, Philip Burton, Bacup, Ray Bott, Chester, Glyn Matthews, Kendal, Paul McFadden, Warrington.

NORTH EAST - Pages 107 - 123
Maureen Ellis, Leeds, Amy Walton, Otley, Elizabeth Haines, Shipley, Lyndsay Hall, Halifax, Steve Sneyd, Huddersfield, Linda Copley, Bradford, Pat McKenna, Hartlepool, Stacy Akers, Bishop Auckland, Sara Newby, Darlington, Christine Robinson, Peterlee, Isabella Veitch, Berwick, Sheila Stephenson, South Shields, James McLeish, Washington, Pauline Thompson, Gateshead, Louise Shepherd, Newcastle, Bill Elder, Bridlington, Lucy McCollin, Hull, Jean Oxley, Scarborough, Patricia Pearson, Selby, Candice Jones, Northallerton, Alan Glasby, York, Michael Bramley, Skipton, June Long, Thirsk, Glenn Granter, Barnsley, George Burgin, Rotherham, Rebecca Wolman, Sheffield.

SCOTLAND - Pages 124 - 131
Christina Anderson, Inverness, Gillian Robin, Strathaven, Shona Ritch, Orkney, Marie Hunter, Edinburgh, Sheila Munro, Dundee, Albert Gamage, Irvine, Jenny Chaplin, Largs, Tim West, Stonehaven, Cate Campbell, Aberdeen, Michelle Melville, Fort William, Andrew Burnside, Falkirk, Jack Pollock, Glasgow.

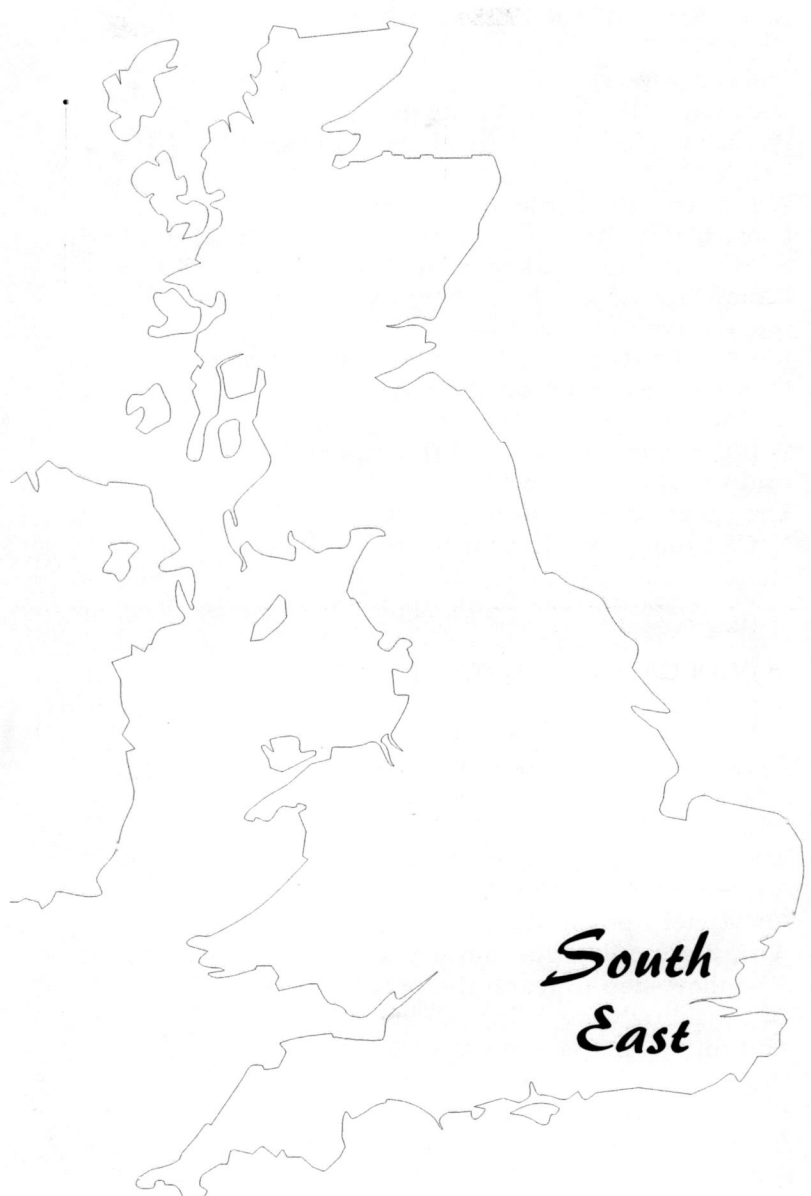

BSE - NOVEMBER 1998

The controversy rages on,
They say BSE in cows - has gone,
But bear this in mind - go back 13 years,
Before CJD, before the tears,
Why blame the cattle and the sheep,
I say, blame the Russians because they could not keep,
A lid or sarcophagus on a nuclear disaster,
From Chernobyl, where they say, they master
nuclear power, from where caesium is born,
Blown from the East - the West saw the dawn,
Our fields were poisoned by the winds,
And we all know the Russians sinned,
Will there be an end to all this fuss,
And will the world ever trust,
The things that scientist will say,
Not for tomorrow, but for today.

John Harper Smith, High Wycombe, Buckinghamshire

ROMAN GARDEN-MENTON FRANCE

A broken jug, a tiny shrine
To gods of other days than mine.
A lovely vase upon its side
Whose beauty was the potter's pride.
A marble slab upon the ground,
A group of olives planted round.
A shepherd boy in dappled shade
With flute to lips that never played.
A shallow step to reach the pool
Of sparkling water, clear and cool.
And round the pool, mosaic tiles
Of trees and birds and crocodiles,
A curling snake, a fearsome dog
A scorpion and a jumping frog.
A hundred steps of gleaming white

With urns of flowers on every flight.
A terrace covered by a vine
With purple grapes for summer wine
Where dark-eyed girls with braided hair
Brought bowls of fruit for all to share.

    Louise Rider, Amersharm, Buckinghamshire

ETERNITY

Eternity, not a big word,
But the meaning immense,
I can honestly say,
To me, it makes no sense
the concept too great,
The notion profound.
How time just goes on,
While the world turns round.
The enormity of space
The universe so vast.
But, be honest,
Surely time, can't last
What comes after?
Please explain,
Perhaps we all just live and live again.

    Ellen Potter, Milton Keynes, Buckinghamshire

LOVE MUST WAIT

How sweeter is the love
That comes with mellow years:
The ripened fruit, more succulent,
That hangs upon life's bough.
If only I had learned of love
The things that I know now.
The flush of youth no blessing brings,
And in me finds no favour;

11

A richer thing I now possess;
A finer joy I savour.
For love must come of age, like wine,
Full bodied and mature;
Then love will overcome all else
And finally endure.

Neil Innes, Buckingham, Buckinghamshire

THE OAK TREE

As I gaze upon its majesty
My heart is filled with pride
For its presence here has surely blest
This our countryside
For if I could have chosen
How to adorn this land
It would have been with the mighty oak
For nothing is so grand
To think that from an acorn
This lofty giant can grow
Man is filled with wonder
On how this can be so
Think about its power
Swaying in the breeze
Be in awe of its splendour
This giant among our trees
And when life is weary
And becomes too much to bear
Remember all this beauty
That we're allowed to share.

Val Harvey, Chesham, Buckinghamshire

THE TIME HAS COME

The time has come to open your eyes.
It's time to see who you are.

It's time for shadows to fall behind,
You are a shining star!
The time has come for you to smile
And wipe away your tears
The time has come for you to change,
To eradicate your fears.
The courage comes from within your heart
It's been there all along.
It's time to accept and start again
The time has come to be strong.

Alexandra Singleton, Welwyn Garden City, Hertfordshire

INVISIBLE

Seen, but never noticed
She fulfils her daily tasks at work,
Uncomplaining,
Never going sick,
Never making waves.

Until,

The day she decides
She's had enough of the routine,
Of the boredom, the tedium.
Leaves without prior warning
No longer invisible.

Joyce Walker, Borehamwood, Hertfordshire

EGO

Reception at street level counts on facts;
there's system under unshadowed light, a cool air
of reason and control; the display units there
face faces quite as bland; a smile corrects
all thoughts of arrogance, impatience or lax

management, fosters belief that my well-being's their
career,
and that the bowels of the business are what I see here ...
no hidden designs through deep-laid ducts.

But somewhere, I know, sits a creature pondering me:
upstairs or down, in a shadowy, littered place,
whose purposes, imperative as gunshots, cross my own;
who orders the shapes and weights which cleverly
disguise while keeping substance, till purpose has a grace
that humours me, yet guards his dues and sanctions, every
one.

Phil Heath, Letchworth, Hertfordshire

GROWING

Don't tell your child to 'sit down' on the bus,
He doesn't understand
He will not want to 'sit and be quiet',
It's much more fun to stand.
And if he falls and hits his head
He'll cry and then he'll know,
Be there to pick him up
But don't say, 'I told you so.'
Because he's learnt a lesson
By making his own mistake,
Life is a hard school
But the child will bend, not break.

Lisa Chandler, Basingstoke, Hampshire

THE OLD SAYING GOES

The old saying goes,
"It is better to have loved and lost than never to have loved
at all."
But, why, for once, can't I love and keep?

Why is it, that once again, my love is lost and I am left alone to weep?

I have cried a river of tears, deep enough to drown in.
Why is it, that in the game of love I am always the loser, guaranteed never to win?

Countless times I have had to pick up the pieces of my broken heart.
I don't know if I can do that again.
I am not sure I can make another fresh start.

      Sarah Brown, Aldershot, Hampshire

MEDITATION

The wheel it spins
The fool looks on
Its rim speeds heaven through its course,
The spokes they shriek and flail and creak
The hub is still at peace.

      Kevin Moylett, Southampton, Hampshire

TIME

Dear clock upon the wall that takes my gladness
And turns it into language of your own,
How know you of my inner self that races
To keep in step, with pleasures lightly sown?

Hours that pass as minutes lightly fleeting
Their birth remembered in their sudden death.
You grind away on wheels no time to linger
For us poor souls, who try to keep us in step.

When life is as a bird and sailing upwards
You speed me on to end my flight of bliss,

When sadness calls you drag her in to linger
And hold her by the hand for me to kiss.

Days and hours divided into minutes
A game of draughts upon a checkered sea,
But still you guard your secrets softly purring
Amongst your wheels of brass, away from me.

     Audrey Cameron-Cowburn, Gosport, Hampshire

HARVEST

On and on and on, it goes from me comes
back to me, always continuing ever round
and bound to be forever,
sealed in the shine of a star,
held in the crystal's eye,
in the space that holds this world in place
from the orb that lights the sky,
ever onwards the spirit flies and cries
it's tears of peace,
to all of those who hear the words that
love is sown to reap ...

     Mark Smith, Bordon, Hampshire

MY HIGHEST

I crouch on my knees by the large door in
The side of the plane, the instructor buckled
To my back tells me to fall in three.
'One!' he shouts down my ear, I feel the coldness
Of the swirling wind bite through my clothes
And make my skin pimple.
'Two!' I begin to feel the tight panicky
Feeling hit my stomach like never before,
A surge of immense fright and suspense clash
Inside of me to make one undescribable excitement.

I know this is it, no way back.
I feel my whole body quivering, but then the fright
Is gone and the reality takes place.
'Three!' my whole body falls, I see the ground
Below me coming nearer and nearer, slowly but
Surely. The wind rushing to meet me. The
Excitement a rush that I will never forget, I
Wave my arms out in the air. An uncontrollable
Force taking me, and that's when I feel my
Highest.

Lucy Vaughan, Alton, Hampshire

THE WIFE

My wife is giving me jobs in the house
There's more than I though to being a spouse
I must ask if she'll give me a rate
But working for nothing seems to be my fate
What with cleaning, dusting and vacuuming too
I hardly have time to go to the loo
She shouts and bosses and says what to do
I'm sure she thinks I haven't a clue
There's much more to housework than I thought
I'll soon need counselling as I'm overwrought
I'm not allowed to speak or say a word
Just to be seen and not heard

Brian Dennis, Biggleswade, Bedfordshire

A MYTH

'Oh for the good old days I hear some say,
Then, seldom time for play.

No warm clothes, just rags to beat the cold
No central heating when Winter took its hold
Funerals galore employed the aging Rector

Infant mortality was then a raging spectre.

Now running water's there, both hot and cold
No need to go barefoot as they of old
Medicines secure infant survival
Thus giving Rector time for a revival.

A myth, the so called 'Good old days'
Now days are golden in so many ways.

Dolly Harmer, Leighton Buzzard, Bedfordshire

THE AMERICAN MILITARY CHAPEL (CAMBRIDGE)

The ceiling's mosaic flights face squarely east
And cut a path through history's drifting sands.
Airmen, who gave their lives to fight the beast
Fly home above wide, wild uncharted lands.
Their engines whine and make a thunderous roar.
Fine vapour trails mark every fiery path
As the heroic air-fleet bestrides the distant shore
And all the stars of morning shine and laugh.
The chapel walls reverberate with praise;
Their windows glow and boast the names of states
While honour sparks a thousand joyful lays
And valiant souls sweep through celestial gates.
Through the earthly gates passes a GI bride.
She weeps and prays, then smiling leaves with pride.

Dennis Mabey, Bedford, Bedfordshire

RAIN

Do we like rain?
It's such a strain
What no sun - they look in vain
What do we gain?
Life's such a bane!

Hear it rushing, gurgling down a drain
Or pitter-pattering on a window pane
Those sounds that drive some folk insane
But in the main
I won't complain
I love it!

      Pat House, Thatcham, Berkshire

DREAM PRISON

At night as I look into the starry sky,
An image appears way up high,
Of someone who is locked behind bars,
Someone that I cannot reach,
To let out and welcome into,
My world of living dreams,
Where life's mysteries don't cease,
And our existence is not quite what it seems.
Dream on, you may find peace!

     Amanda Sanderson, Newbury, Berkshire

BIRTH
Soft in the emerging light
of our first dawn
You arrive
Effortless
Confirming my imaginings.
In countless dreams
I've seen your face
Heard your cries
Stroked your downy head
Smelled your warmth
And felt your tiny fingers close on mine
All this time
Confirming my imaginings.
I've known at least a

part of you
But more than that
I'll never know

Judith MacBeth, Reading, Berkshire

MY FATHER'S HANDS

I have got my father's hands.
Not quite as large
nor with the span
that measured
far, far better than
any other
I had known.
Those hands have now
become my own.

Pamela Gardner, Maidenhead, Berkshire

MY JOB

It's Monday again I'm up at six
On goes the kettle for my morning fix
Off I go in my car
I've looked at my rota It's not too far
There's Annie, and Winnie and Mark too
These are my clients, just a few
Sometimes they're happy.
and sometimes they're sad.
But when I arrive they seem quite glad
I help them wash and also dress
and sometimes even clean they're mess
But I'm a carer, that's my part
and all you need
Is a great big heart.

Carol Sutherland, Windsor, Berkshire

VIAGRA MAN

You can call me viagra man
I couldn't make love
But now I can
I just pop in a pill
And off I go
Steady at first, just do it slow

Build up the pace
Keep going for hours
Made the wife tired
So I bought her some flowers

So now when I make love
I just pop in a pill
And the wife, she's just sat there
Writing her will.

Keith Strangwood, Banbury, Oxfordshire

IMAGINATION

Imagine a world where children are dying
from famine, starvation, imagine the crying.

Imagine a world where children see killing,
Imagine their minds, all terror that's filling.

Imagine a world where children are screaming
at night, in their beds, from the horrors they're dreaming.

Imagine a world where children addicted
on drugs, from conception, their parents inflicted.

Imagine a world where children abducted,
Abused and misused, their whole world corrupted.

No need to imagine, that world is today,
Imagining won't make it all go away.

Imagine a world where every child smiles,
And every child laughs, every day, all the while.

Imagine a world where every child's prayer
is answered, and they are protected with care.

Imagine that world, it is there for the taking,
If we can undo the mistakes we are making.

> *Jim Sargant, Thame, Oxfordshire*

CHURCH ON THE HILL

In stated arch medieval, inspiring within reach
Apostles ever-changing, extending Gospel preach.
Downward step eroded, onward aisle explore
Mystery in aura, sculpture to adore.
Landlord of the building, he you came to see
Inwardly apparent, to those that bend the knee.
Fount of given vision, circled in stained glass
Suffer tiny babies, initiate the past.
Hymn the one creator, visible in mould
Glory and contentment feature in the old.
Ages fix united in a common prayer
Praise from pews related, deity uncompared.
Candles flicker singly, gutter in the void
Ageless as a symbol, pinnacle uncloyed.

> *Kenneth Webb, Bicester, Oxfordshire*

THE HOSPITAL VISIT

When I open the curtains - how will you be?
Should anything happen, they said they'd phone me.

You were asleep when I left, so weren't aware,
When I brushed from your face a tendril of hair,
And put back the ward seat on a stack of three.

In daylight, I'll look out and once again see
The familiar front garden, the green cypress tree,
The grass, and the flower-beds that long for your care.
When I open the curtains.

Will I tomorrow still talk about 'we',
And get back to our ritual of five o'clock tea,
Then afterwards watch the programmes we share
From our settee and matched easy-chair?
If only I knew how you will be,
When I open the curtains.

T Robertson, Abingdon, Oxfordshire

TURNING POINT

Strung up, unstrung, unravelled
pulled by need, drawn out
by cold withdrawal pangs,
craving her more than caffeine,
he strides the darkening streets,
winning her back the one fixed point
inside his spinning head.

His journey ends. She's gone
before, into the wintry night
alight with the same flame
that burns in him. They crossed
unseeing in their paths,
apart, yet bound together. He turns.
His journey home starts here.

Dympna Pyle, Henley-on-Thames, Oxfordshire

SUCH LOVE

John Three, Sixteen, those precious words.
We all know to be true,
For God so loved the world, We read
He gave His Son for you.

For you, for me, for everyone
Our Dear Lord Jesus died,
His blood was shed for all of us,
And no one is denied.

He knows what lies within each heart
He's saddened when we fall
But he gently lifts us up again.
And helps us to walk tall.

He's always there to guide our steps.
He'll listen when we pray.
Such love, too wonderful it seems.
But it's there for us today.

Jean Gray, Eastbourne, East Sussex

ACCIDENTAL LOSS OF A POEM

My poem surfaced in a bathtime soak.
The words swirled in my head in soapy streams
And stretched out like the long brown curl of hair
My fingers found along the smooth bath side.
I scooped the pools of watery wanderings back
Into the oily tub.

The ideas rose above my head in steam
As I soaked and sponged my sleepy night-time skin.
Alliteration fixed them in a frame
Before they vanished down the overflow.
How did the struggling frantic scrabble go?

I wrote it down before I went to bed.
But sleep drove every memory from my head.

Next day the 'masterpiece' had disappeared
Possibly decomposed and forming dust
An instant recycling of confused ideas.
I gave up looking and wrote this instead.

> *Claire Shelton-Jones, Brighton, East Sussex*

BANNED SUBSTANCE EUROPE

There's a product on the market
Usually meant for kids
It contains the risk of BSE
A sort of CJD confetti
The Europhiles have gone and banned
Alphabetti Spaghetti!

> *Neil Dickson, Hove, East Sussex*

IF FALLING LEAVES SPELL YOUR NAME

If the sky looks nice
Don't ask what it means
If the snow blocks your door
Don't ask why
If I get sick
I won't tell anyone
Don't make a fuss
When I die

> *Kay Green, Hastings, East Sussex*

THE SANCTUARY

Such foolish imagery upon the mind.
Meteor of love's arcadian thought

That casts aside the saner kind,
And drowns itself in dreams it wrought.
And these lost dreams shall dreams remain,
Marionettes of the soul's behest
That delve the deep to love reclaim.
To live in peace and sleep at rest.

Sally Selmes, St Leonards-on-Sea, East Sussex

OPTIMISM

Tiny pinhole of twinkling light:
A prism of a million shades.
Colour sparkles into every corner,
The sombre world begins to fade.
Illumination all around:
Dusk vanquished by triumphant beams.
Beneath the surface full of soot
The grin of hope discreetly gleams.

Tanya Stephens, Dartford, Kent

UNWRITTEN

I found your pen today
in my desk drawer
hidden among the cheap
blue biros, pencils and paperclips.
It caught me by surprise
nestling there in all its golden glory,
two black unbeating hearts
upon its pocket clip; your initials
on the barrel shot clean through me,
and I could not swallow the nugget
of memory stuck in my throat.
The smoke from your illicit cigarettes
stung my eyes, making me blink back
the moist joy of your smile, the rarity

of your anger, the pleading
of your last sullen silence.

I never did say goodbye properly
and sometimes I can't even remember
just how long you have been gone,
but the pen still writes
as you sign your name gently
in teardrops on my cheek.

Carole Blacher, Orpington, Kent

WILL THE SUN RISE TOMORROW?

In Druid days, the Autumn haze,
Would lead the priest to prayer,
And with sacrifice and revelry,
Beg the sun come back next year

But when we found, the earth was round,
The sun doesn't rise for man,
But pulls us round his sphere,
We understood the season's plan.

Yet man, too small, still views it all,
As if the sun comes just for him,
He counts two thousand years, and harbours fears,
The sun will leave at its own whim.

Christine Finnis, Maidstone, Kent

DESTINY

Through the open window from the bustling square,
Comes the fragrant summer air,
From a vista lost in time's passing cloud,
That winter shadows will forever shroud.

Scenes lie dead like Autumn leaves,
And the book of destiny flutters in the breeze.
Across its pages the meandering roads leads,
In Summer's chapter lie the scattered seeds.

Footsteps tread the path of fate,
Beyond the rainbow the shadow of futurity waits,
But the bird of freedom southward flies,
For your blue eyes told me erstwhile lies.

Ghosts wandering silent and unseen,
Under the canopy of the silver moonbeam,
They tiptoe softly by that sweet stream,
Haunting shapes in the elysian garden of dreams.

In the twilight hours I met your wraith there,
By the colonnade, under the winding stair,
You gave me one sad regretful glance,
And around the shimmering fountain others now dance.

Eleanor Marshall, Gillingham, Kent

ECSTASY

Flying.
Flying,
Soul bright
To the crystal light.
No rejection
No pain
In the velvet wind
And diamond rain.

No shame,
No fear
In the pulsing heart
And shimmering tear.
Here,

Here,
Spirit flight
In the black night

Dying,
Dying.

                              Diane Watson, Dover, Kent

THE BADLANDS - CALGARY, CANADA

Like bridal veils or cascades of cathedral spire
These cruel crusts,
Like croutons at a brunch,
Denuded against the sky
Yield sifted soot of terracotta spilled.
The mineshafts, left long ago as ghosts,
Wade in their water
And hip-like hills
Pulse in our person.

                              Nola Small, Bromley, Kent

SEPARATION

We are penguins and polar bears apart
You and I
Things dear to me mean nothing to your heart
You don't cry

So I'll go my way
You go yours
Me on w e b b e d feet
You on all fours

FOR WE ARE POLES APART

                              Joan Croft Todd, Chislehurst, Kent

MILLENNIUM

Do shadows creep this silent quarter
Searching for an open door
When once the new millennium take

And in this murkey twilight
Will the engines roar
To still us as they did before

Those darker thoughts that linger here
Bowing to temptation's bliss
With promises of time's dual face

Yet musk this fools decay
With fingers blooded by the toil
Lie ghosts of a new age.

      Cye Thomas, Chatham, Kent

ROMANCE

As we hid in the woods
I suddenly realised
That I love you.
As we played like children
I remembered why I love you.

When our lips brushed together
I knew that,
From then on
I would always, love you.

      Chris Lee-Rowden, Whitstable, Kent

CHRISTOPHER

Christopher hangs

with a wry smile mystifying
his dead countenance.

You clever clever man.
Christopher if you could
only see us now

You would grimace.
You're heroic, you're mad,
Christopher you're dead.

Gavin Rodney, Uxbridge, London

CEREMONY OF EARTH

Remember man that you are earth
And to the earth you must return
For earth is moist and dark and fertile
Without a root the seed will burn
So love your home, your hearth, your money
Work the garden, plant the seed
Pluck the fruit and taste the honey
Then you'll never be in need!

Peter Burns, Ealing, London

OBLIVION

She glides across the sand, flowingly,
Yet still leaving a faint imprint of feet.
As she walks through the unchanging scene,
The salt spray whips her flaxen hair,
Stinging her face.
Her footprints sink behind her,
Sink into the sand,
And into oblivion.
Her shadow, distorted and never-ending,

Stretches into the unknown,
Waiting, watching for her.
She wipes away a salty tear.
Turning without warning
She looks back along the trail of prints,
Fading fast,
And with a sigh, she continues
On her final journey,
Into the swirling blue depths.
She does not falter
Or once look back,
As the serene waves carry her
Into oblivion.

Nicola York, Wimbledon, London

WATCH THIS SPACE

An Autumn park poem?
All the ingredients are here:
Alert eyes, itchy fingers, ready pen, empty bench ...
A park with usual 'furnishings':
Patient fisherman,
Dutiful mothers, playful children;
Dogs exercising their owners:
One a white Highland Terrier (the dog)
Joyfully discovers a pool of melted chocolate.
A pristine Chow struts his stuff;
A 'Jesus' duck shows off ...
A flotilla of Canadian geese sail the lake;
A fountain calms the ears,
A bountiful sun
Bestows diamonds on the water;
A gentle breeze soughs through the trees;
It rains cornflakes,
Ummm ...
Watch this space!

Joy Lennick, Romford, Essex

THE TEAR FROM MY HEART

When you kissed that tear from my eye,
I knew we were deeply in love, you and I,
We promised each other that we'd never part,
Because that one little teardrop came straight
From my heart.

When you held me close in your arms
I knew the sweet allure of your charms.
We loved each other right from the start,
Because that one little teardrop came straight
From my heart.

When you said that you would be mine
We sauntered through life in a manner so fine,
Knowing that nothing could drive us apart.
Because that one little teardrop came straight
From my heart.

But along came another who took you away,
Nothing I said would induce you to stay,
For you the time had come to depart,
Because you'd forgotten the teardrop that came
From my heart.
Straight from my heart.

Mary Baird-Hammond, Chelsea, London

AMAZING GRACE

Amazing what that child could do,
A little girl of almost two.
So easy to lose, too hard to find;
You'd think she was following close behind,
And then you'd hear a frightful crash,
The milk bottles on the step she'd decided to smash.
Or it would go quiet around the place,

And you'd think you'd searched every possible space.
When in the larder you'd finally meet,
She'd be biting each cooking apple to find one which was sweet.
She squirted toothpaste all up the wall,
And used soap to plug the sink and make a waterfall.
In the summer when it got really hot,
She poured flour on herself so that "she was not"
But at the end of the day you couldn't be mad,
'Coz she was just inquisitive, not trying to be bad!

Verity Burgess, Chelmsford, Essex

THE NEXT MILLENNIUM

As into the millennium, we are about to enter,
Let us all, with peaceful thought centre.
Christianity has been with us, for two thousand years,
It is our beliefs that help us, through our fears.

Life without it, where would we all be,
Without God to call on, the God we can't see.
God all around us, see's all that we do,
God never deserts us, God sees us all through.

And if for a moment, we think we are alone,
And our fears all return, and our hearts feel like stone.
Take a good look, and say a prayer, to God up above,
A prayer to our God, a God full of love.

V M Foulger, Canvey Island, Essex

IF MUSIC BE

Musician keep on playing and don't you end the tune
returning me to here and now
returning much too soon

Timing stored in memory
etched in tapping feet
springs music's reincarnation
In the rhythm of the beat

In the swirling of the dances
in the old familiar scene
In the magic of the orchestra
in the half forgotten dream

So musician keep on playing
let the rhythm flow
A serenade to yesterday
And my youth long ago

Betty Davis, Southend, Essex

CONVERSATION WITH A BUSKER

'The tool of my trade,' he says,
'is vermilion, varnished, pear-shaped,
well-strung.'

'When I play,' he says,
'bloodspots appear on my fingers,
signs of stigmata,
or a woman's menses.'

'I know how to fake orgasm,' he hums, arpeggio.

'And by the end of a set,' he says,
'my bones have hardened, whitened,
my heart is hard-core ...
I want to bury my head in the pillow, of course.'

'I know the score,' he says,
'exposing my throat to vampires
night after night.

So I eat garlic bread
and breakfast alone.'

'Yet when I play for myself,' he says,
'I carve my initials into wood
with a penknife.'

Jean Owen, Westcliff, Essex

BLURRED VISION

Alien life forms committing crimes
Inside my body.
Body invaders draining my senses,
All except feeling.
Feeling a life but not mine own,
Indulging in affliction.
Affliction belonging to me, splitting waves
of agonising torture.
Torture unable to be recognised
By the eyes
Eyes which only experience the outside
of functioning humanity.
Humanity, frightened, mentally
runs from sanity.
Sanity I longer possess it was
stolen by damage.
Damage to the soul and body I once lived in.

Beverley Cope, Wallington, Surrey

SUDDEN AND INFECTIOUS FEAR

Sudden and infectious fear
This cruel confrontation with life
Commands and regulations; control
Lists of words in precise alphabetical order
Comply, deny, empathise, infuriate.

Twisted dreams of a can of cider
Beckoning my unkissed lips ...
Caressing my unusual personality ...
Things to be added, things to be taken from me ...
Incisive agitation, slitting my voice
As I have balded my arms
Insignificant matters, so vital ...
Persist with your direction
Life has little worth
Without your skills.

Kate Crowther, Godalming, Surrey

INSOMNIA

I lay awake
It's the dead of night
Yet still I can't sleep
I'm filled with fright.

I hear a tap on the window
A creak on the stairs
It's freaking me out
Although no one is there.

Eventually I sleep
But I have a bad dream
I wake up to darkness
And suppress my screams.

I leave on the light
But still feel insecure
I don't know
How much I can endure.

I shut my windows
And lock my door
And dread the feeling

That's coming back once more.

Juliette Seel, Morden, Surrey

AT THE THOMAS HARDY MUSEUM, DORCHESTER

Without, all's well; 'tis high July;
Within, the mood is cold;
a score of bowed heads strain and sigh:
some fair, some sad, some old.
From far and near they've heard the call
to come and praise their God.
But is it he, up on the wall,
that gloomy-looking sod?

Dr Andrew Cunningham, Guildford, Surrey

WINTERLIGHT

Let us this December night leave the ring of heat, The lapping flames around the fire's heart,
Move with bodies tensed against the light
Towards the moon's pull and the cloud's hand.

Arms of angels hold us, lend our bodies
Height of stars and the planet's whirl,
Grant us sufficiency of light so we may enter
The twisting lanes to lost villages.

So we may stare in the mirror of silent pools
By long-deserted greens, deepen our sight
Of what lies beyond the things that seem
And make our vision clear as winterlight.

Barry Tebb, Sutton, Surrey

SWALLOW SUMMER

Wheeling, and gliding, the swallow feeds.
Sweeping up the insects of flight that he needs.
Mouth agape, he vacuums them in.
Lunchtime to be held on the wing.
This migratory bird fills up the skies,
across the countryside, once Spring arrives.
Favourite congregational habitat on a farm,
preparing a nest site on the ledge of a barn.
Two broods of chicks will be raised in a good year.
After which, these versatile fliers will appear;
on overhead wires, in flocks chattering.
To gossip, on their last gathering;
before heading off again to find the sun,
where in another country, Summer has begun.

Jane Eagle, Radstock, North East Somerset

TAXI CAB ON 8TH AVE

And I am searching through this window
For you.

And you are consumed in the belly of the beast
that is the city.

And I see you walking in your unhappiness
that is me.

And your heart is breaking under a bloodshot moon
in his petroleum sky.

And the city dwindles in my distance
yet you still grow.

Andrew Nash, Bristol, Avon

A LETTER FROM A FRIEND

On a murky Monday morning, under a sullen Stygian sky,
I glare through the front-room window. God! I wish I could die!
Here comes the postman up the path. More bloody bills I guess!
But no, there's only one letter, and the envelope's address
Is penned in an elegant unknown hand. I'm puzzled; who can it be?
There's only one way to solve it: I open it up to see,
Look at the missive inside it, and ... oh! It's a letter from you!
And the world becomes a different place; it takes on another hue
As I call to mind a smiling face and read a message that clears
The sombre humour from my soul. The darkness disappears
As I turn to my desk, pick up my pen, and write this hasty reply
On a matchless Monday morning, under a sapphire Summer sky.

Peter Lewis, Bath, North East Somerset

THE SMILE

The unexpected things in life
jolt me. The soft nest of wool
in the blackthorn, the thunder
cloud which pounces from behind
on a Summer's day, your smile
when you heard I have cancer.

That smile, swift and secret
but no less real for that,
The same smile you smiled

when Simon phoned to say
he would visit while I
would be away.
That selfsame smile.

Tony Cloke, Okehampton, Devon

SLOW DEATH

Keep on performing, I can't do it
I'm ungrateful and I'm bored.
Why do you come? What do you want?
You've taken all of me and you still, want more.

Ridiculous disguises, agony behind the mask
My character gets harder and harder to play.
I'm not big time person, we're not a big time band.
Music's no fun anymore
- suicide may be the only way.

Chris Bond, Exeter, Devon

ANIMAL HUSBANDRY

baa, baa black sheep
bullied in a field

oink, oink fat pig
poked at during meals

moo, moo stupid cow
ridiculed in the yard

ignorance in packed animals
makes being different hard

Peter Atha, Paignton, Devon

MEMORIES

And reaching for the long-lost days of my childhood,
remembering the happy hours so long ago;
where we used to play all day, laughing, in the wood
amongst the trees, branches hanging low.
I'm yearning for the days of my joyful childhood
when I did no cares or sorrows know.
Bring them back I cry; if I only could!
Why, oh why did I have to grow?

Victoria Ewan, Torquay, Devon

ROUGH STUFF

The professor sat down
and spat out
legions of half truths,
and they fell around his feet
like dead sparrows.

He said
"It is everybody's God given right
to walk through the hills and woods."
Then he squealed
"I am tired of walking on tarmac"
and he headed for the rough stuff.

I say
rip up the cobbles,
smash up the steps,
and place a thin sliver of hardness
through the wilderness,
then we may talk to each other calmly,
without me
biting off your head.

Martin Wildman, Newton Abbot, Devon

INTUITION

No gossamer arranged
In haphazard massed cascades,
Or grass appearing from the earth
In ever different blades.
No moted shafts of sunlight
Gently drifting through the air,
Can touch the textured shadows
That flow softly through your hair.

No sapphire crystal facet
Slowly 'wakened by the sun,
Or dancing liquid rainbows
That laughing downwards run.
I'd have to be a prophet
Or a watcher of the skies,
To plumb the hidden depths
That lie so secret in your eyes.

A R Bradbury, Salisbury, Wiltshire

THE RIVER'S JOURNEY

I start my journey up in the hills,
From some unknown source,
I start on my course,
Cascading and foaming,
Down cataracts bubbling,
Crystal - blue clear!
As my course takes a change,
I am now twisting and turning,
Meandering through meadows,
Enriched with flowers and birds of all species,
Snaking through fields and towns.
And on, silently, I roll.
I am old; no longer a lively stream,
But a slow, wide, tidal river,

Now,
The oceans await me,
But who knows what secrets may hide?

                              Simon Russell, Swindon, Wiltshire

NIGHT LIES

At night we'd stare into the sky, looking for answers
to questions we could not comprehend.
It made us feel small.

You unloaded your worries and I listened,
my ears your greatest comfort.

I liked to listen.
Your insecurities were bigger than mine.
You could never face life alone
and I was a willing shoulder to cry on.

At night your fears grew.
Plenty of room for them to expand
in the sky above our heads.

I never once complained,
content to bury my anxiety
whilst driving yours away.

You made me feel sane,
my grip on reality much stronger than yours.

We were true friends
prepared to lie to each other
but only under the cover of darkness.

                              Jerry Toman, Camborne, Cornwall

LATE SPRING

"Come", you said, "and let us walk
Together. Let us dance and talk.
It will be good to remember
In other years. A fire aglow
Around which to gather the last late primrose
Of Springs so long ago.

And for all the times that have passed
Beyond our reach or reason, now at least
Let us sip the Autumn wine pressed
From sour fruit that suddenly sun ripened.
Let us count all the precious hours
The golden flowers we have won."

So I will take the first sweet step
To walk again as though we had first met.
Knowing that Life is a rare, rich wine
To be sipped to stop the speeding hours,
To be gathered like a wreath for living
Of all the Springtime flowers

Barney Hill, Redruth, Cornwall

ANDY GOLDSWORTHY (SCULPTOR)/LAND ARTIST

Chasing the slow landflow
leaving a trace of man;
a rain shadow recorded, on
the surface of stone or sand.
White pebbles broken
reveal a snake of black;
unleash dark energy
hidden beneath the cracks.
Waiting for moonlit water;
fire in setting sun,
the magic light of moment,

with a camera won.
Slate built arches in fields
window the soul of the land;
earth evokes a meaning
spirit understands.

Josie May Hodges, Bodmin, Cornwall

SHEARING DAY

Sheep with eyes like drugged hawks,
    stonily stare
As shears snip-snap;
    shed their weathered pride.
Supine, they slump
    like lumps of lard,
Forelegs hung as a shepherd's crook.
Backs gripped twixt thighs
    strong-thonged in leather.
Shorn of the warm cream fleece,
    some tarred and torn,
They bleat, peer in frantic fear
    as they are heaved, stomach high
To straddle on shaken hooves
    the new smell of themselves
Before heavy calloused hands
    clumsily thrust one on another into pen,
Then to struggle, a huddle of shanks
    to a field's freedom and noontide's
    sun-sweet young green grass.

Janine Vallor, Bridport, Dorset

CONCERT AT CRICKET ST THOMAS

The sheep are grazing still, high on the hill,
As the sun slips silently across the valley,
Illuminating worn stone

And spot-lighting layered firs
And an ancient oak on its cropped lawn.

A helium heart dips in farewell
As it dances up into the late sun.

A bird, displaced, flutters
As it surveys its uninvited guests.

The sheep are leaving, drifting off
Silent as spirits between the darkening trees.

Dorothy Davis-Sellick, Poole, Dorset

HARBOUR

Ludicrous likeness,
Sea sound to cow bell,
The dull metallic clank
Of sheet on mast.

Slip slupping slop
Of tide on tethered hull.
The gulls are sleeping
And the children gone.

At last the orange sun
Slides into smoky gold
Abandoned, vast
The dappled beach is empty.

The fishermen are out,
Nosing towards the channel.
This is their morning
As their day begins.

Elsie Torrent, Bournemouth, Dorset

OUR CHILDREN

Mum, dad, please can we have,
Constant chattering, nag, nag, nag.

Depending on you for their every need,
Looking for guidance, following your lead.

The laughter gathered from the things they say,
Feeling of pride and joy, through the achievements of each day.

Through them your own childhood relived,
Memories of times in your past, vivid.

Inherited traits, personality and looks,
From us their parents, these things took.

Our lives enriched, from the moment when,
We brought into the world, you, our two children.

Susan Amos, Cinderford, Gloucestershire

HELP!

"Hello, I'm fine," Is this me,
Am I the person that you see.
Look in my eyes, do they shine,
The smile I'm smiling, is it mine?
I need hope.

Do you listen when I speak,
Am I strong or am I weak,
Never have I asked for care,
Shouldn't someone just be there?
I can't cope.

I'm looking for a place to hide

To let my loneliness subside.
Catch me please before I fall,
I seem to have no strength at all.
Cast a rope.

I'm shouting 'Help' without a sound,
Before I'm lost will I be found.
When passing strangers say "Hello"
Yet never knew me, do they know?
It's no joke.

Are they the ones who'll take my hand,
Ask no questions but understand
And make me strong and coax my mind
To rise again and somehow find
Utopia?

Marj Phelpstead, Gloucester, Gloucestershire

ABOVE LAKE LOUISE

If a person wanted to guruflect
to the Great Spirit
here is a shrine to water.

We climb to a high place,
kneel down, lips wide open
to the first beestings of water.
The spring, like strings at the back of a piano,
tinkles long-forgotten tunes, Chopsticks.

Beneath us, the wind sweeps
through the tops of trees, firs and tall pines,
making the air resinous above them.
It ruffles the turquoise lakes
and the deep chalky blue of Lake Louise.

Here is the lost innocence of water.

Our predatory lips thirst for more and more.
If each drop could quench the five thousand.

Michael Henry, Cheltenham, Gloucestershire

MOTHER EARTH

Fears of war and world pollution
We will cause our own destruction.
Global warming, acid rain
Starving children, wracked with pain.
We just can't see
What's clearly there
And do we even really care.
Think of your children,
It's their world too,
Let them grow in peace,
And love to protect our earth,
For years to come.

Belinda Harris, Chard, Somerset

SUNSET

The sun falls gently from the sky
People evaporate like mist
Ice cream and hot dog stands must close
And sandcastles wait for the tide to kiss.

Fading shadows on the sand
A pinkish hue lies on the sea
The yachts white sails have turned blood red
As another day prepares for bed.

The sky is streaked with crimson light
like golden angels still in flight
And as the sun dips in the sea
The twilight falls surrounding me.

And as I stand between dark and light
Soon to glimpse the stars at night
I know with enormous certainty
That God created you and me.

The sun has set, but will soon arise
Tomorrow again it will light up the sky.
New hopes - new dreams will be upset
The only constant sun-rise sun-set.

Tom Sage, Frome, Somerset

SOUL'S TRIUMPH

I hold no fear of death,
No terror haunts my soul;
Lay upon me every wreath,
When every bell can toll.

For now I know, am certain, sure,
That when my eyelids close,
To slumber then, and stillness lure
Myself in rapt repose.

In life each morn my sights reveal
The incandescent dawn;
Across my shoulder light beams steal,
Awakening of morn.

In death each day my soul shall rise,
As spirit's eye sleeps on;
No movement quickens, hear my sighs,
Awareness now is gone.

As a teardrop or of rain,
They kiss the leaden earth,
There I lie, in death's domain,

Awaiting my rebirth.

Lynda Dickson, Taunton, Somerset

DARK SHIP

A dark ship sails across a silent sea.
No lanterns shine, from topmost spar to hull.
With windless sails and rudder drifting free,
Alone and empty; echoing and dull.

Each island passing by, ablaze with light
Has happy houses offering good cheer;
Gay conversation; friendly smiles bright.
Warm welcome for the dark ship coming here.

But watch the hands that sweep. Beware the chime!
For after but a little lapse of time
The conversation strains, the smiles fail;
No welcome now, and so the ship must sail
Alone again across the silent sea.
Alone the dark ship sails. Alone, like me.

Alison Ashby, Yeovil, Somerset

TIME OUT

Here I clear my head of thoughts
not wanted, of my working day.
This is a quieter place to be
and take it easy. Play
sweet music to touch my soul.
As a crooner sings, her melody brings
a longed for peace within the whole
of my body. I sigh
and let the noisy world pass me by.

Here in solitude I stretch

and let the warmth invade my limbs.
All is silent now, as I relax
my mind and body. Hymns
poetry and songs I mutter
in an under-tone. Here away from 'phone,
from people, idle thoughts flutter
through my head. I laugh
and add more hot water to my bath.

Paul Tipney, Bridgwater, Somerset

HE IS THE KEY

HE is the key, He is the key,
Jesus brings us liberty.
All power's in His precious name,
How can our lives stay the same.

His Glory shines through the earth,
In flowers, mountains, even birth.
So please don't tell us there's no God,
We didn't evolve from a fish or frog.

We were predestined long ago,
He loves us more than we will know.
For each have sinned and that is why,
Jesus came to testify.

To break the bondage of our sin,
And have the power flow within.
His gift of life is completely free,
So we may share in His victory.

Kay Willding, Pontypridd, Mid-Glam

CHEPSTOW

Touched by the rivers Wye and Severn,
Chepstow is my idea of heaven.
There's no need to go on holiday when you live in a town like this;
Just to be resident here, throughout the year, is my idea of bliss.
The countryside, and waterways, that lie within our reach,
Have far more attraction than some sleazy Spanish beach.
The local shops cater for all our wants and needs,
Food, clothes, furniture, even a packet of seeds.
It's small enough that to give the impression of living in a village,

But large enough that you have no need to go off and rape
and pillage.
I wasn't born in Chepstow; I came here quite by chance,
After more than thirty years, it still has me in a trance.

>   Geraldine Parr, Chepstow, Monmouthshire

CANA

It's just a shell now is Cana
The pulpit's gone, no thunder from
The polished oak, glass fronted pulpit.
No pews where once sat in silence a
Black-dressed congregation of quietness.
No wine, no breaking of bread,
No service for the passing dead,
No blushing bride in virgin white,
No harvest suppers, no pleasing sight.
The Sunday School has long since gone,
There are no throats filled with song.
The lights are dimmed, just dark despair,
No one it seems gives time to care.
The hall is silent as the grave,
The vestry to have nought to save.
Silence now is all that's left.
An empty space without a guest.

>   Derek Morgan, Aberdare, Mid-Glamorgan

DISPOSSESSED

Half the world's in boxes on the path.
The other half's already disappeared.
Furniture gone, you take a last look.
Bright patches hurt the walls where pictures were.
Bare windows seem enormous; sockets stare.
The real shape of emptied rooms surprises:
A new perspective has estranged all you took

for granted. Yes! Suddenly so much space.
So clean, so bright. An ideal place for kids
you might have wanted. You cross the flat
to check the horizon you both saw has really gone.
Of course it has: the contract's void.
Now, time to go. But where? You turn.
And bang. It hits. You're naked as a bulb
without its shade, shocked by its own stark glare.
Suddenly aware how floorboards stripped of carpet
amplify each single step; you freeze:
just stand there staring down a telescope in reverse
watching yourself shrink to a child.
Your head full of voices.

Maggie Bevan, Colwyn Bay, Clwyd

ETHIOPIAN GOLD

It was a night of revelation,
Passion coursed through my veins,
Cataracts of electricity giving substance to my soul,

and, the cherry trees wept,
along the avenue.
Where the tributary coursed,
into the gutter,
a mobile of tins, sticks, whirling, eddying
and the Gods, sounded a distant rumble.

A crash,
and then, "Mary Shelley,"
Found her "Beautiful, Great God,"
as the lightning streaked, alive and dangerous, wondrous
to me.

and my five pound note,
fell from my fingers,
falling,

While I mesmerised,
watched my paper boat, float,
bobbing into the sewer.

and, the rain fell,
"Great God,"
Like Ethiopian Gold.

Helen Miles, Bridgend, Mid-Glamorgan

AL AND MOLL

Our "Al" went and bought a doll,
That looked just like a gangster's Moll,
With bright red lips and body bare,
Because he was desperate for a bit of spare.
The man in the shop said "She's quite real,
Brimming over with sex appeal,
She's just like the real thing,"
But Al wasn't sure where to begin,
He lifted Moll out of the box,
Then gazed upon her golden locks,
He then began to blow and puff,
When fully inflated she wasn't so rough,
Then he began to stroke her hair,
And ran his fingers everywhere,
When Al decided the time was right,
She gave him such an awful fright,
Moll was so real it couldn't be true,
For when he said "I'm gonna love you, "
This voice screamed out as there he sat,
"I've got a headache - so you can forget about that."

Rebecca Rees, Ammanford, Carmarthenshire

DAWNING WONDER

I close my eyes and weep, upon him death does creep
looking lovingly on his face of old

So many times his laughter has banished the cold
I take his hand and cry knowing that he's going to die
His time has come he needs God's rest
He deserves the very best.
Come my child come to me
I've come to take you home, where freely you can roam
Open your eyes my child
Don't be scared I am here to eradicate your dying fear
Father is it really you
Yes take my hand my son your work here has been done
God takes him by the hand
To welcome him to his eternal land.
He opens his eyes and looks past me
What is it that he can see
A dawning wonder in his eyes
Such a heavenly surprise I close my eyes and weep
As death no more has to creep

Samantha Crofts, Cardiff, South Glamorgan

THE ECO-WORRIER

He wears corduroys
And a pinstripe jacket.
He bought them from a charity bazaar
He looks bizarre.

A face pinpricked with jewellery
Sideburns fashioned to a point.
He wears his hair in dreadlocks
And smokes a long fat joint.

He drinks his beer by bottles
And raves about the trees.
He cares nothing much for money
Just enough to buy his needs.

His girlfriend she wears camouflage

And hides out on the streets.
She sleeps upon her Issues
And pops her pills like sweets.

They worry about the future
Ours or theirs I ask?
Because they're too stoned to notice
Their future's in the past.

Neil Cunningham, Tenby, Pembrokeshire

SENSES

Have you seen the sea lapping
so gently on the shore,
The sun glistening on the crests
As the breakers gently roar?

Have you heard the birds singing
bringing in the dawn?
It makes you feel so very glad
That there's another morn.

Have you tasted the sweet water
that comes from the mountain side
Tasted the honey from the bees
And fruits from far and wide?

Have you smelt the sweet flowers
of pink, blue and red,
And the glorious smell of
newly baked bread?

Did you touch your child's hand
As he lay in his bed,
The feel of soft fur
As you stroked the cat's head?

Patricia Newton, Caerphilly, Mid-Glamorgan

STAR CHILD

From a butterfly's wings to a hurricane.
Take a cup and drink, turn off someone's rain.
Every thought in your mind, every word you say,
Changes your life forever, changes mine a little more each day.

We are all one, one is what we are.
You're in every grain of sand, you're in every shining star.
Each breath you breathe, your first and your last,
is the one given to us by all that has past.

Each second that passes has gone before
we circle and return to a child forever more.
With time-machine eyes we view each sun.
Our watch hands grasp on eternity has begun.

Don't think that you're alone,
Don't think that no one cares.
Don't think that there's no truth
No beauty or elegance.

This world of mine was built by design
Nothing was left to chance.
Within this chaotic, spiralling universe
is a poetic, balletic, music driven dance.

Leslie Grice, Burton-on-Trent, Staffordshire

IT'S JUST A JOKE

"It's just a joke!" she said one day
As she got dressed to go away.
"We have a conference to do
Three days and I'll be back with you.
I'd better go. I can't delay."

So much he wanted her to stay;
When she had gone his world turned grey:
Could what she said to be really true
"It's just a joke?"

Next time the "conference" was May:
Three days he tried his best to pray;
His heart was full because he knew,
When she returned, that they were through.
No longer did she laugh and say
"It's just a joke."

Dorothy Thompson, Stratford, Warwickshire

FOOD FOR THOUGHT

What shall we have for dinner?
Bacon, burger or beans,
Or maybe we'll grab a take-away,
A favourite of the teens.

And I'm reading all the labels,
To make sure it's GM free,
What's hydrolysed vegetable protein?
I think I need a degree!

And there's E numbers, colours and flavours,
What on earth is it all about?
Mom never had this trouble,
Of that I have no doubt.

In her day 'twas good old meat n' two veg,
No pizzas, paellas or rice,
And for pudding, dad's favourite spotted dick.
On Sundays he'd have it twice.

At last I think I've found it,
No monosodium glutamate,

But, oh dear! I'll have to look again,
It's three weeks out of date!

Annette Jones, Cannock, Staffordshire

LIQUORICE ALLSORTS

Soft, 'rolypole' barmaids, in pink and blue
blouses
everyone's favourite, soft sweet and yielding.
Thin, flattened spinsters, with tightly permed hair.
Blue and pink rinses, covering centres
of prejudice born in age old resistance.
Hard black original, needing no icing
scornful to join the blacks with white centres
in their Babylon box, not sure of their culture
coffee and white, mixed up idealists.
Though black is beautiful, colourful mixtures
purists declare, can only decay.
Without the black, the mixture is bland
a melting pot mix of colourful parts
sweet outside layers, pastel and pretty,
hiding the hardness of liquorice hearts.

Bobbie Dee, Leamington Spa, Warwickshire

HOLIDAY BULGE BLUES

My holiday was wonderful,
The foreign food was great!
I swallowed lots of alcohol
And ate and ate and ate!

Back home again, my clothes were tight,
The zippers wouldn't meet!
Thick rolls of fat obscured my view;
I couldn't see my feet!

My photos came, of sun-drenched views,
But how they made me glum,
For most were dominated by
My belly or my bum!

It's great to go on holiday,
It's good to self indulge,
If only the result were not
A fast-expending bulge!

And so I'll count the calories
Until the moment when,
Bikini shaped, I'll pack and go
On holiday again!

Sue Minton, Rugby, Warwickshire

MAD DOG AND THE ENGLISHMAN

Sprawled out
with the sun and the breeze
at my beck and call,
I share my day off
with my dog.
We take it easy - or so I thought.

So easily, teasily
goaded into action by:
the chewing of my trainers
the chewing of my pen
the licking of my face
the wearing of my sunglasses (in her mouth)
the collapsing on my poem
the mad turn round the garden
her panting and her ranting and her shameless gallivanting.

Chasing the shadows
from the washing line

I play up with
this mad English dog of mine.

   Spencer Winnett, Stourport-on-Severn, Worcestershire
LOSS

Do you think that, in a darker moment,
When they held hands, and saw the future
As a threat, they agreed that if one went,
The other wouldn't want to live
To face a lonely world?

Or, did each think that thought, stay silent,
And not put it into words?

Now, we'll never know - we've lost them both.
As friends, we all must feel: if only
We'd been there, to share the moment and the burden,
We might have helped to ease the stress.

Now, we who're left are lonely.

And amongst all the memories of 'gentle', 'noble', 'good',
Is the aching loss of 'used to', 'was', and 'were'.

   Robert Collins, Hereford, Herefordshire

THE AFTERMATH

Come let us celebrate the peace, my friend.
Our battle's over, fighting's done.
It's rumoured in the halls of power that you and I have won.
But what? Won what?
What are the spoils that we have gained?
What is the victor's prize for which our blood was drained?
The papers claim in banner headlines clear
That you and I have saved mankind from tyranny and fear.

It's rumoured in the halls of power these words are not sincere,
That there is nought to cheer,
That we were tools, misguided fools,
Who fought a worthless fight.
Let it be said, though sheep misled
We thought that we were right.
We thought and fought and then we died, believing in our cause.
Oh let us rest in peace, my friend, and scorn all false applause!
It's rumoured in the halls of power that men still plot their wars.

Patrick Rooke, Evesham, Worcestershire

CRACK OF DAWN

Will you be up
At the crack of dawn
When church bells ring out
Heralding Christmas morn.

Will you be up
At the crack of dawn
When Christmas wrappings
Get ripped and torn.

Will you be up
At the crack of dawn
When new bikes
Get ridden over frosty lawns.

Will you be up
At the crack of dawn
Or cosy in bed
With the curtains drawn.

Ann Weavers, Kidderminster, Worcestershire

THE GRAIN STORE

A grey light matched the mood of the room
through sashes, Welsh-damp as drizzle
against settled, doleful walls, sat
waiting the fall of self-dereliction.

I had seen it handed round,
from the graceful parting of an old family,
to the merchant's artless stripping,
to the crowbar of rot, the teeth of neglect,
the plaster jigsawing then slowly undoing.

Grain now covers the oak-board floor,
tied sacks bubbling up to the mantelpiece,
not a fire crackling in arpeggios
as a welcome home. No one,
not a soul now comes and goes,
but the ghosts of guests in Edwardian dress,
in silent, mock disbelief.

Matthew Thomas, Ludlow, Shropshire

A BEDTIME PLEA

Don't leave me here in the dark,
Don't leave me here all alone,
Just give me your hand to hold please
Until I'm safely asleep.

I dive on my bed at night still
In case there's something beneath,
There's no escaping that tingly chill
That something might grab my feet!

Monsters comes in all shapes and sizes
And not in the way you think.
Those shadows that lurk on every corner

Prevent me from sleeping a wink!

They're crafty creatures it seems,
They make me cold with fright,
Just a figment of my dreams
They still make a chilling sight!

That's why the child inside me
Needs to hold your hand tight;
To have you always beside me
And banish all fear from my night.

Akkeber Osborne, Telford, Shropshire

SNOWBERRY

Pale silver dancer,
Pirouetting at my midnight window,
Ensnaring moths and moonbeams
With a delicate outstretched paw.
In moon's full light
Soft gleaming, like aurora borealis,
Throwing choreographed feline shadows
On the polished oaken floor.

Isobel Stone, Shrewsbury, Shropshire

HAPPINESS

Rip away your weeds and float in your flowers,
Blow away your clouds and feel the sun for hours.
For laughter in the sunshine is as easy as it seems,
Oblivion in blissfulness, in your joyful whispered dreams.
Aspects of life, once so bleak, seem better now than ever,
So keep smiling on and your happiness, will last in peace forever.
So sing a song and be free, grin and then be mellow.
Link hand in hand happily, every foe, friend and fellow.

Drift away from worries, turmoil, grief and strife,
For this world is now so beautiful, as I lead this carefree life.

                    Craig Welburn, Whitchurch, Shropshire

COMPARED TO YOU

I've seen the Northern lights
From the Southern Hemisphere.
Seen a comet's flight so close, so near
Shooting stars traverse a star clustered sky,
Saw lightning strike make might - 'day bright',
Seen Jupiter rise, and mercury fall.
But compared to you I'd seen nothing at all!
Seen all the wonders of the world
or so I thought!
Been to the depth of the sea,
'Alone just me!
Seen beauty abound only in nature to be found,
Thought there be 'nothing new', then I met you!
The essence of life, of love shown true,
You're presence so near - my life's search here
finally my destiny so 'clear'.
All this new to 'I' with confidence high.
To have survived alone of all I try,
Now, the truth finally comes through.
I had known nothing before I 'knew you'!

                    John Cooper, Stourbridge, West Midlands

THE WHEAT FIELD - 1920's

Glinting in the late sun's glow
A swelling, golden sea of wheat,
Each heavy head sways to and fro
And the air smells very sweet.

Rippling in the silver moonlight
With dancing, whiskered silhouettes,
Whispering on the still of night
Sharing the harvest mouse's secrets.

Comes the dawn and early rising
Harvest helpers to the field,
Fine the weather for the scything
Plentiful, the good earth's yield.

Shimmering in the heat of day
The harvest prayer is granted,
Carefully tended in every way
Since the seed was planted.

Now 'tis time to down the tine
The stook to lean back on,
To disband, with cheese and wine
And make merry, the day is one.

Jo Rosson Gaskin, Solihull, West Midlands

DYING BUSINESS

You ignore the pleas and cries,
At the loss of fragile life.
The young snatched from their mother,
So we can milk her dry.

Her young dragged away,
Shoved in a plane,
By a corporate bastard state
That wants its monetary gain.

Dumped in a strange land,
Shackled in a crate.
No solids in their short life,
Pain and torture is their fate.

You ignore the pleas and cries
of the masses with a conscience,
They call it a democracy
But veal is still a dying trade.

   Kerry Ann Lewis, Wolverhampton, West Midlands

TEMPTATION

You come to me when I am alone
Sweet venom, bitter antidote to my
weak and desolate soul.
A pure silken glove which prods and probes
and pollutes my mind
with thoughts that soothe, then sedates
all sense of rationality you find.

I know you now, seed of that exotically
wretched and tangible deed.
Planted in the bed of curiosity, you feed
upon my doubts.
Within the confines of my mind you grew,
blossomed and bloomed
and bore the fruit I all too readily consumed

   Alice Smith, Birmingham, West Midlands

PICTURE POSTCARDS

The days are sunless
Seasons fail to exist,
All but the sharp sting of Winter,
A dark cold mist lingering through empty streets

I am ignorant to the sun,
Yet it exists in my mind,
Forever teasing me with ice cream van melodies,
Painted smiles stretch on a bed of blue blameless seas

The unspoilt beige surface I scarred without a care,
I have to confess - the sun was my witness,
And it was only then when I stared into the bright nakedness
That it blinded me with disillusionment

As I walk through streets of lost shadows
Feeling the pain of each footstep revisited,
Strangers pass, eyes radiant and illuminated
At the sun, but they do not see me in my darkness

Endless days of perfected routine
Haunt me like a stuck record
Waiting for the sun to welcome me to its colours
But from here the future doesn't look bright

Marie Evans, Coventry, West Midlands

I TRIED DRUGS

I stood at the door of hell
There was no knocker or a bell
It opened wide, and fear I felt
If I linger here, I will melt.
So bright. So very hot.
Do I enter. I think not
If it's heavens gates I want to see.
I must give this world the best in me.

Anthony Mace, Stoke, Staffordshire

EVERYTHING'S PERFECT UNTIL YOUR TAXI COMES

Tonight's the night I might
just stop hating myself
Somehow I'll gurgle happy without
walloping my bile straight down the flush
Since I packed up the lighter fuel, ooh days ago now,

I've stopped stomping on old Bill Wordsworths'
untenable visions of perfect yellow, and agreed,
that yes I am a wobbly human who needs to be adored
By your twist and leap kisses slippy with this downpour
postcode that makes you and I very suicidal,
The spunky monk with his go-away face writes a poem
with a laser beam covering all the unusual themes
Like fresh buttered bungalows perched well past the
patches of black eyes and chunky sarnies with your folks,
He calls it 'everything's perfect until the taxi comes'
and as it pushes back into goodbye I feel tremendous,
shocked

Matt Nunn, Sutton Coldfield, West Midlands

VISITING WOODS

I know these woods where gentle folk
Live simple lives; early awoke
By birdsong and a crowing cock
They fill the air with morning smoke.

It rises above the paddock
And drifts over fields of livestock
Between the woods and fishing lake
Where water birds and boatmen flock.

I know the woods where clearings break
The dark deep paths you have to take.
A wilderness I know lies there
A journey I so often make.

These woods I know I have to share
Though visitors are truly rare
Just those who live beneath the smoke,
The gentle caring country folk.

           Graham Smith, Kettering, Northamptonshire

DO IT YOURSELF

DIY man Derek Moore
Came home early to check his door
He'd only hung it the night before
Saw strange shoes upon the floor
Heard his wife cry out "more, more"
Went and got his power saw.

DIY man Derek Moore
Peered around the bedroom door
Saw wife and neighbour in the raw
"The central heating works, for sure
but they'll drag those units to the floor"

he flicked the switch on his power saw.

DIY man Derek Moore
Covered in blood and guts and gore
Smoothed the concrete basement floor
Leaned smoking on the louvre door
"At least I'm rid of that crushing bore
but I'm going to miss the man next door."

Martin Heseltine, Lincoln, Lincolnshire

FIRST LOVE

First love, like a young fire
burning in your heart
when romance is fresh and hot

The hot thrill of your kiss
sharp tingling, body sparks
the scent of your body
waft on a zephyr

Your smile enraptured
by the colour in the sky
hold me, kiss me, touch me
turning through the pages
of our unwritten love

Making love, intersperse with fantastic beauty
enveloped in a lasting love

Your ecstacy lifted me, into the sky
we'll ride a rainbow, a cloud, a storm
flying on a carpet of gold
together forever.

Gary Wright, Gainsborough, Lincolnshire

ABSENCE AND THE FOND HEART

My love, he is so far away,
So how can it be so?
He pulls hard on my heart strings
And I cannot let go.

I can't believe that life goes on.
To me, it's standing still.
I miss him so much every day,
And think I always will.

I feel like half a person,
The other half detached,
And connected to my soulmate
To whom I'm wholly matched.

I know I'm very lucky though.
This pain won't last forever.
He's coming home in two weeks time.
At last! We'll be together!

Linda Moore, Scunthorpe, Lincolnshire

ONCE

He was once a doctor,
Cured a thousand souls or more,
But the ravages of time spare him not one iota in recompense.
The hands which held out the bawling babe to tired, happy arms of love,
Shake helpless, useless by his side,
Not even the sense to bring spoon to withered lips.
His "carers" offer little dignity to this plastic-panted professional,
After all, what dignity is left, only that captured in photographs and certificates on walls?

Not apparent as it once was.
But still, inside, behind the eyes,
He clings to what once was, to what he was, Once.

Louise Law, Louth, Lincolnshire

A WAR CHILD

The wailing of the siren
Drags us from our bed
Half asleep and fearful
As down the road we sped
Quick into the shelter
To keep us safe from harm
We see familiar faces there
All showing some alarm!
The muffled sounds of bombs above
Will we still have a home?
Or could our friendly little home
Be nothing but a load of stone?
At last the long night is over
We've made it through once more
Rays of dusty sunlight
Struggle through the door
The "all clear" has just sounded
Nothing more to fear
Our home still as we left it
Oh look our mum is here

Betty Clark, Skegness, Linconshire

BY APPOINTMENT

Dear 'Guardian Angel' of the medical surgery
Pray listen as to you I make this plea
Myself being an aging man of little wealth
Who is feeling slightly jaded in his health
Do hereby ask your aid to stem this grievance

By allowing me an appointment, with Doc Stevens
Who in the course of time, I feel quite sure
Will provide me with a most effective cure
By giving my aged body some defence
Against bugs and germs, at minimum expense
Most any day of week will suit me fine
But the hour I would prefer is just on nine
A time you'll no doubt agree, most civilising
When others of my age group are but rising
Thus allowing me that most deserved luxury
Of avoiding any other mad old fools like me.

James Smith, Chesterfield, Derbyshire

FOR MY SON IN HIS GRIEF

How can I not share your pain,
I who bore you in my womb,
carried you in my arms
and hold you always in my heart?
Too old for me to kiss it better now,
I see you walking with your wound
and I can hear
the silent, tearless weeping in your heart

Anne Shimwell, Bakewell, Derbyshire

WE WHO ARE LEFT

It is the little things that we remember
heads bowed, in the damp light of November
the way they looked, chins up and heads held high
marching off to fight the foe beneath a foreign sky
Those of us who watch with rain stroked eyes
still see their khaki'd arms bid last goodbyes
whilst those of us who stumbled on
in frost rimmed mud,
tasted mustard's sting, smelled old blood

that dried upon the cold and stiffening limbs
and brought the flies to settle
on the chest propped chins
now stand and wear our poppies,
stiff with pride,
remembering little else but those who died

Sheila Sharpe, Derby, Derbyshire

SPRING

The fire was blazing brightly,
The rain was teeming down,
A draft blew through the window
and knocked the flowers down.
I donned my mac and wellies,
took my brolly from the stand,
to take the dog for walkies
over wet and soggy land.
I trudged through cold wet puddles
while the dog trailed far behind,
the rain ran down my back and front
into places hard to find.
The wind blew round my head and ears
and caused a gentle tear.
The day has been a rotten one
and they said that Spring was here.

Patricia Wells, Matlock, Derbyshire

A PROMISE TO ALL

In the sky so way up high
a vivid rainbow delights the eye.
Beautiful shades, seven there be
merge into one richness to see.

Bright these colours to bestow

a promise to all such peace does flow.
Moving so gently as we glance
enchantment there, the prisms dance.

To the side so very near
a true reflection pastel hues cheer.
Glorious vision to enthral
such harmony beyond recall.

Red, orange, yellow divine
green, blue, indigo, violet fine.
A wondrous picture to perceive
tomorrow's hope, always believe.

Margaret Jackson, Swadlincote, Derbyshire

BEGGAR

An old man outside a closed down shop,
Wearing army medals with a hat on top.
A cold cup of tea in one hand,
His only possession an elastic band.
Reading a week old paper,
Telling a week old news.

Daniel Morley, Ripley, Derbyshire

15'S CANDLE

A candle now flickers,
Like the dance of a soul,
Calling and drawing me,
Devouring me whole,

With her mesmerising aura
She captures my mind,
"Step into the future,
Leave your shadows behind,

Trust to me your dark pain
I'll transform it to light,
I'll change the cold doubt of your day
To the warm faith of night,

I give you my promise
Of a love, forever to cherish,
I give you my strength to go on,
Until the demons, inside of you, perish."

Then I stir from my trance:
I'm alone once again,
The candle now silent
Against the scream of my pain.

Heather-Julie Hollingsworth, Coalville, Leicestershire

MONSOON

The clouds gather ominously in a corner of the sky,
A brooding tension fills the air. As if all are waiting
For deliverance, renewal and hope to fly,
The wind builds and builds its keening;
And there is a moment of breathless stillness.
Suddenly they come raindrops of grace,
A shower of blessing. The air is so fresh!
I let the cool rain envelop my face.
The parched earth gives a fleeting scent
Of thirsty leaves, grass and wet clay,
The smell elevates our enjoyment
In the reviving rain I dance away.

Priya Chauhan, Loughborough, Leicestershire

CIRCUS ELEPHANTS

Field full of elephants shackled to the ground.

Majestic animals no longer so proud.
You roamed across the wide open spaces,
But now freedom's limited to three small paces.

Kaye Axon, Leicester, Leicestershire

SEASONS

Young tender leaves unfurl
Brilliant in their newness,
So green and fresh.
The diamond dew sparkles
In the first light of a new day, born of love.
Here it begins, yet unspoiled.

The golden glow that nursed you into life
Is now white-hot with a new fierceness,
She draws the sap from the fine lacy web
Once spun in her security.

Gentle green is now bronze and gold,
A burnished glory
Before the cold harsh winds
Whisk the frail frame into dust.

Teresa Shelton, Retford, Nottinghamshire

DISTINCT IMPRESSIONS

Distinct impressions no
longer acquire validity.
Presumption is the
only necessary qualification.
How judgmental and
incorrect can they be?
How passive and inadequate?
What rights do they have
to assume such

unorthodox ideals.
To suspect me of
unobliterated happiness.
To be "A-OK".
Hunky dory.
Groovy.
Whatever.
Envious of their ability to
be open and outspoken.
To gush with emotion.
To sob with conviction.
To laugh like a hyena.
Instead I smile through gritted teeth
Gnash my lip to prevent
rolling tears.
And trap my emotions
like wind in my
stomach.

Vikki Styles, Nottingham, Nottinghamshire

LEAVING

The dying sun splashed gold across the hills,
And tranquil waves became a sea of flame,
And one by one the stars came out to say farewell,
As though their diamond splendour eased the pain!

Far islands shimmered in a violet haze,
As darkness overpowered the fading light,
Salt seawinds keened and sighed among steep, grassy braes,
Soon all the world was cloaked in velvet night.

The quiet burn swam slowly to the sea
Where foam-edged wavelets fretted on the sands,
Pale, rising moon peeped shyly through the trees,
And silvered all the earth with loving hands.

I recall the magic of the clear, star-jewelled light,
And the whispers of the fitful, gentle breeze,
Telling me the dawn would break and end the dream-clad night,
Saying it was time for me to leave

Another place, another time when sunset gleams
I drink the wine of memory, and while I sleep
I sow fond thoughts of home that I may reap
A richer harvest of forgotten dreams.

Edward Mitchell, Corby, Northamptonshire

ALONE

A smile can change a million frowns.
A laugh lifts up a desperate soul.
A hug can let me know you care,
A kiss can pull me from the hole.
A hand reached out to help and hold.
A heart to tell me all is well.
Is someone there, when I'm all alone
To save me from my inner hell.

Elizabeth Morton, Wellingborough, Northamptonshire

THE DYING FIRE

Summer - the dying fire in Autumn's hearth
Dies for a day, then splutters another
Last flame out of the season's aftermath.

Loose leaves of red and brown absorb the heat,
And try to cling another day for warmth,
But burn into the grass and scald the street.

Then we smell the smoke that curls and turns
Its way from gardens as the burnt-out leaves

Are raked together and their brownness burns.

Dominic Allard, Northampton, Northamptonshire

TOO LATE

I stayed away from home for years
Time passed swiftly by
Till one night, clearly in a dream
I heard my mother cry,

"Oh son come home return to me
Forgive what I have done
I love you so, I always will
My precious wandering son,"

I made up my mind up to go home
To the mountains, and the vales,
I'd go back home to dear old mam,
Back to my native Wales,

I pictured mam's sad smiling face,
I saw her joy and tears,
The longing burned within me,
As it had throughout the years

I drove on through the valley
Reached the cottage gate
Then something told me in my heart,
I had returned too late

Campanula May Downes, Bury-St-Edmunds, Suffolk

VIEW FROM THE 50A ON A WINTER'S MORNING

In the fields the dawn eyes are blazing;
A mimicking, spherical attraction like the profound rising sun.
All around, a toffee filled sky melts upon the trees and beneath,
Sugar tipped blades of morning grass stand abrupt;
A dusty regiment.

Yawning trees receive another day.
Capturing the moist air on their branches they become veiled,
like an old man's skin in a storm.
Flecks of charcoal sheep breathe frosted air,
exhaling clouds like waking dreams they gaze, encrusted,
by the riverside.
And the glassy road, entwined like fallen ribbon lays
captive by the fields,
As they lead, like a religion, to an influx of day.

Sarah Stone, Cromer, Norfolk

IT'S THE MAXIMUM, THE MINIMUM, THE MILLENNIUM

It's the maximum, the minimum, the millennium.
It happened before, A thousand fears or more
Before 1066 and the Scots and the Picts,
Before the Yankees decision to loose nuclear fission:
The Angles, the Jutes and the butterfly position:
The Plantagenets, the Tudors and Hanoverians:
Before steam trains, computers and such
Before Ford motors and the mechanical clutch
We danced, we showed, banners were unfurled
God's in his heaven, all's right with the world.

Norman Mitchell, Downham Market, Norfolk

SUNLIT UPLANDS, THE END OF THE ROAD

Life is a struggle,
A constant, unremitting struggle,
But the road leads on
To sunlit uplands;
Or so I have believed.

And so it is.
They stretch before me now,

The sun shines down
But on a bleak landscape,
Swept by an icy wind,
Heavy with menace.

In the distance,
Across that bare, forbidding plain,
I see a little knot of people.
I feel I know them
But their backs are turned.

      Donald Watts, King's Lynn, Norfolk

LOVE LETTERS

Now the moon
is just a memory
of the night before.
Like those unfinished
love letters
Washed away from on
the shore.
Love letters are my words
to say I love you
As the stars above look down.
But her eyes will never see
them now
or even understand
why I went to all the trouble
to write love letters in wet sand.

      K Lake, Great Yarmouth, Norfolk

EMPTINESS

There is only silence and emptiness now,
No glaring banners of how you lived your life
Criticising ... spying ... prying

Forcing you into a corner ... crying.
Pleading to be just left alone
Wanting to call your soul your own.

No more running of hungry feet
Panting down the hostile street
They corner you ... like hunted prey
You hide ... you try to get away
Too many ... too many from which to hide
You are engulfed, like turning tide.

We are all guilty of wanting more
than you should have had to give,
The secrets behind your closed door
and how your short life was lived,
Should not have been for public view.
If only we knew ... if only we knew ...

Patricia Rudduck, Parson Drove, Cambridgeshire

ALL I AM IS A SERVANT TO MY GODDESS

I am nothing except me,
I have no talents but use to my capability,
I worry about nothing,
Only I am totally devoted to my Goddess,
Naked, I kneel to serve her,
I claim no possessions nor land nor clothing as my own,
All belongs to the Goddess,
I seek no desire but to drink juice my Goddess provides,
Surplus poured from her body,
I would use my tongue to wash her, devoutly serving her,
I would become her footstool,
I would worship her and serve all her angelic children,
All I wish is to serve her,
My drink would be her released fluids, once she's drank her choice,
Food would be from washing her,

Home would be her lower parts, my bed would be at her feet,
I would cherish her image,
Whilst on earth and heaven hereafter with my naked soul.

Louis Barrow, March, Cambridgeshire

THE STRAWBERRY

The strawberry is Summer's temptress,
Who brazenly shows off her curvaciousness,
And simply lives to entice
A ravenous lover, who'll never think twice
About sinking teeth into such succulent flesh.
To appease, a sudden hungriness.
The hussy when lifted stands proud
Above the leafy bed where rampant runners crowd,
Indifferent to her promiscuousity
And her wanton generosity
In flaunting her form, before the lover she's enticed.
Who stands transfixed! Openly salivates, and doesn't think twice
About plucking, and sucking, in all her ruby sweetness.
With lips lingering to prolong the kiss.
Before his smouldering passion ignites,
And she is consumed in one blissful bite.

Diana Moules, Wisbech, Cambridgeshire

LISTENING

He stands,
Frail on failing legs,
Swaying his shuffling feet
Padding the floor.

Earphones askew
On his old man's face

His wrinkled features twisted
with secret feelings.

The orchestra swells
in his dying brain.

Rosemary Westwell, Ely, Cambridgeshire

IF ONLY THEY KNEW

He sees her, he knows her, he loves her,
But afraid to tell her.
She sees him, she knows him, she loves him,
But she's afraid to tell him.

What can you do?
What can you say?
If only they knew,
They would be together today.

For he's afraid, and so is she.
For he's in love, and she is too.
They both have told me, and told me not to say.
If only they knew,
They would be together today.

Janet Cross, Peterborough, Cambridgeshire

A SECRET PLACE

Bent low,
sometimes crawling,
knees hurting,
hair snagged.

Under branches,
between stems,
reaching for foot-holds,

gripping the roots.

The bank falls steeply away,
down to the river below.

Working along,
holding on tightly,
on level ground
by a gnarled tree trunk,
the canopy of leaves
cool and dark,
green and calming,
far away from the world.

The retreat of my childhood ...
a secret place.

Ann Bennett, Haverhill, Suffolk

THE COLOUR OF THE WIND

The wind the colour of translucent butterflies' wings,
of poppies shimmering in fields of heat.
The kitten clouds, fluffy and white
skim along - foam filled waves.
Laser beams of sunshine, flicker between the trees,
while the silent secrets of the moss
spring between the feet of million year old stones.
The doubt, the uncertainty, the soft kiss of the breeze
amid the tall venerable gentlemen
reaching their arms to the warmth.
The cool shadows, reservoirs of change,
Offer sanctity, peace, tranquillity
Altering the colour of the wind.

Val McCurdy, Lowestoft, Suffolk

RUN FOR COVER

Crashing through the front gate, screeching round the path,
Falling through the kitchen door, landing on the mat.
Heading for the bedroom like an excocet in flight,
Should I run for cover? no I'll stay and fight!
"Watch that cup of tea now," try and catch that plate,
Guess you're getting old Belle, got there just too late.
Is it a tornado, or a wild unruly pup?
No, it's just the grandkids, come to cheer me up!

Beryl Newcombe, Liverpool, Merseyside

NATURE'S DUDDON BEAUTY

When as a boy I used to play
Upon the Duddon sands,
The sand-dunes, looked so beautiful
'Neath, sunlight's golden strands.

Marram grass spikes, were clumped around
Like, children's unkempt hair,
a straggly line, of seaweed lay
Where, once water gathered there.

Sea-shells lay upon the sand;
So numerous in number,
Like crusted jewels, they lay bedeck,
In ornamental grandeur.

I would paddle in the cool salt sea
And, leap o'er the rippling waves,
There's times, I'd lose my footing?
Then my bottom, came to save!

The sky above, seemed always blue.
Whilst the sun, shone bright and haughty,

When as a boy, I used to play
Amidst, nature's Duddon beauty.

Thomas Graham, Barrow, Cumbria

POETICAL VIOLENCE

I've sold my soul,
(if I have one)
to the words on a page,
to verses that take an age,
to poems built with rage.

I've sold my life
(if it's worth anything)
to the lyrics that I choose,
to the ink that's my bruise,
to the devil in Hai-Ku's.

I've sold my nights,
(if I own the rights)
to the struggle with words,
to a silent plea to be heard,
to severance from the herd.

I've sold my faith,
(if I ever believed)
to this weapon in my hand,
to the bleeding lines I command,
to this hard back cell I'm now damned.

Paul McFadden, Warrington, Cheshire

GROWING OLD

I know I am a super cook
And Sam knows that for sure,
As we've been married for forty years.

Alas! He praises me no more.

I do not mind his lack
Of praise for all I've done;
If only he would sometimes say
I'm still the greatest prize he won.

But then one day young Bill did call
That his wedding, it's fixed for May.
I bustled to the kitchen a cup of tea to make,
And I heard my Sam say;

Don't make the same mistake as me
I've been too shy, not dared to tell my wife
That though she's old, I've never ceased
To love her and shall do all my life.

Sam never saw the tears that spilled
Into that pot of tea I filled.

Bertha Bishop, Lancaster, Lancashire

JUST A ROBOT

I feel just like a robot
I go to bed at ten
Get up early next morning
And off I go again
I toil for many hours
Work hard to get my pay
I go back home at evening
And that ends another day
I'm a good little robot
As I'm sure you'll all agree
But sadly in that robot
where is someone called me

Doris Hester, Blackpool, Lancashire

A TIME AND A PLACE

It could be a crush
At the match of the day,
Or a gunman with a vengeance
Shooting kids as they play.
It could be a slagheap
And a school buried black.
It could be a battered child
Laying dead on the track.

Any event needs
A time and a place;
So they dropped you
An A-bomb,
To wipe the smile off your face.

David Edwards, Ormskirk, Lancashire

HUNTERS MOON

Night came and to the surface of the sea came
He who was to sink and kill and maim
He with streaking wake and hissing decks of foam
Arose and turned towards they who unsuspecting on the
far horizon lay bound for home
For he did look above and see the hunters moon
Which shone out full and bright
And with escorting clouds cast shadows on the sea
And in them hid he from their sight
For hours after moonlight hour and unto day
He stalked his prey that laboured on through mist and
spray
Which hung like shrouds upon the sea ahead
The shrouds that soon would cover they by he cold dead
Now well in range the victim unaware
Awaits the piercing sting and in a blinding flash
A crimson glare

He hears alarm bells ring and sees their rescue flare
The hunters moon now moves from sight
Back in the clouds now black the night
Whilst he now turns to hide back in the sea.

John Bryant, Burnley, Lancashire

THE SHERIFF AND HIS BAND

Once there was a band of cowboys.
They could ride and shoot, and how boys.
They could tame a horse or steer of any brand.
And their tricks with a lasso
Would have astonished kids like you,
And so would have the leader of the band.
He was tall, blue eyed and sandy,
With his fists was very handy,
His fame and smile, were known throughout the west.
Although he was a tough guy,
He never cut up rough, why?
Because he wore a badge upon his chest.
Now, these men of whom I write.
Never known to shirk a fight.
All so brave and bold, have long been laid to rest.
But though they are all dead and gone,
The memory always linger on -
Of the sheriff and his band from way out west.

Hilda Naughton, Colne, Lancashire

WINTER

Winter's here once again,
Bringing snow, sleet and rain,
Day is shortened,
Nights grow cold,
Stars scattered above,
like pieces of gold,

Rooftops, all covered,
Snowdrifts of white.
Glistened on windows,
Ice crystal-bright,
In the depths of the valleys
small creatures they sleep,
Huddled up safely,
from the cruel Winter's bleak.

    Sheila Farrer, Heywood, Manchester

HALLOWEEN

There's an eerie glow in the sky tonight
And it isn't the setting sun
There'll be many a shiver down many a spine
Before this night is done
For tonight is the night when the witches fly
And hobgoblins go out on the town
And the ghoulies and ghosties and long-legged beasties
Spread panic by hanging around
So close all your curtains, and lock all your doors
And fasten the windows up tight
And, whatever you do, never try to find out
What it was that went 'bump' in the night!

    Pauline Barker, Bolton, Lancashire

WINTER MORNING

A cold white world
all colours washed out
blushes shyly pink
to the early sun's caress.

Firmly yet softly
shadows reach out
to hold the land

103

deep in night's embrace.

The white hoarfrost
like a linen sheet
timorously withdraws
under the sun's warm kiss.

The world is revealed
in red and gold and green
dressed to welcome
another Winter's day.

Steve Buttrick, Wilmslow, Cheshire

TV TIMES

Faces
boxed in glass
forever mouthing
the litany of fame
and short success
and the worthiness
of flattery
where nothing matters
but the naming of names
the repetition
of every knowing glance
spun upon the airwaves
spoonfed
to our gaping jaws
and star filled eyes
we collude with their craving
live in the lies
sit in silence
and dream of living

Peter Goldberg, Manchester, Greater Manchester

IF, COME THE HURRICANE ...

If, come the hurricane,
you can sit in your tent
and smile while a caravan
somersaults past your door-flap
you have a touching faith
in the breaking strain
of nylon. Either that
or you're a mountaineer.

                        Philip Burton, Bacup, Lancashire

DANCING EYES

Those eyes that dance in fantasy
Flashing brightly in the light
Pools of magic mystic jewellery
Secret weapon of temptress sultry
That pierce the will of weakened male
And melt away meek shy resistance
Until she has him at her mercy
Pawn of love in sweet surrender
Drawn to trap by dancing eyes

                              Ray Bott, Chester, Cheshire

ELLIS BUTTERWORTH

My name is Ellis Butterworth,
I have a big house up the hill,
I am a pillar of my church,
I am the owner of this mill:

This is a clean and Christian mill,
And Christian it shall always be,
I trust the Good Lord put me here,
But left the management to me:

Each morning, in my business suit,
At stroke of eight I progress in,
Inspect my looms, my men and girls,
Alert for slackness and sin:

No chewing, talking, laughing, here,
This is a place for work not play,
I give my hands a living wage,
And keep them occupied all day.

Each Sunday, in my Sunday suit,
With wife beside I take my pew,
Give thanks to God, and God I hope
Says: "Ellis Butterworth, thank you!"

Glyn Matthews, Kendal, Cumbria

ONE LAST FAG

The day has now dawned, when I have my last fag,
And believe you me, I'll enjoy every drag
I'm having to stop on account of my health
Not to mention my ever diminishing wealth

I'm out of breath, and the energy's flagging
But mainly it's the family, nagging
"You're smoking yourself to an early grave, and think of all the money you'd save"

I have palpitations, and pains in my chest
But I keep it quiet, I think that's the best
Well it's 10am and I'm fair going mad
This nicotine craving is really quite bad
I'll have to have one, be it beg, steal, or borrow
Well I could be struck by a bus tomorrow

I'll crack this addiction to ciggies, I'm sure
But right now this minute, I need just one more
I'll start afresh Monday, I'll give it a crack
But meanwhile I'll have just the odd twenty pack.

Maureen Ellis, Leeds, West Yorkshire

DYING

Someone said
When you're dead
And your heart
Has been bled
And your eye
Holds a tear
Of your fear
Which is shed
And the birds
Round your head

Will cry out
Until fed
And you know
You must go
Head down low
Back to bed
Where you'll find
You are blind
And you'll know
You are dead.

Amy Walton, Otley, West Yorkshire

ON LOOKING AT A DAVID HOCKNEY PAINTING

Strident and shocking
The fiercely red room
Focuses onto the still green centre,
The quiet garden.

In the room
Table, glass, bottle of wine.
Ordinary enough
But tilted a few degrees
To disturb our vision.

Too easy to paint what the eye sees
Any eye
Even the eye of the camera.

A simple enough picture
Colours harsh and brilliant
Furniture turned through an angle.

Now the world looks different.

Elizabeth Haines, Shipley, West Yorkshire

GREAT WATERS DEEP

When my light ceases to exist,
And the flames devour my soul,
Convene the remnants of my life,
Remembering the years, as a whole.
Disperse me in the ocean,
To flow in the waves, to be free,
Pursuing my life through the water,
This place I have longed to be.
Circling within the tide,
Away from such sorrow,
To no longer need to worry,
Of the past, the present, or tomorrow.
When I'm motionless and gone,
You'll find me in the waves,
My spirit in the waters,
These memories, you will have saved.

Lyndsay Hall, Halifax, West Yorkshire

AWAKENED FROM A DREAM

I'm walking along the beach now,
The sand between my toes,
The sun is going down now.
The tide it comes and goes,
An odd gull calls from up above.
A yacht sails out to sea,
A couple passes, so in love,
Oblivious to me.

A shrieking noise comes from afar,
So loud it makes me jump,
It seems to me I'm seeing stars,
I've landed with a thump,
I've fallen out of bed you see,
It makes me want to scream,

The alarm clock has just startled me,
Awakened me from my dream.

Linda Copley, Bradford, West Yorkshire

THEY SAY WE CALLED THEM

The sky is full. Full
of strangeness, yes, but full
too of splendour. The ships
catch sunset as clouds would,
but respond differently, returning not
just colours but music, scents:
imagine warm garlic bread filling
the air horizon,
while songs squeeze all sadness
from us. Ecstacy forever. Conquest.

Steve Sneyd, Huddersfield, West Yorkshire

SUPERMARKET CREAM SPONGE

Coyly you sit in virginal white
A dream of sweet perfection
So creamy and light,
I ache for a bite,
of your delicate confection.

But stop! I'm wooed
by devils food.
Seducer of the slimmer.
Your caress on my lips,
Is a month on my hips
Begone! I will wait for my dinner.

Pat McKenna, Hartlepool, Cleveland

NOTHING

In the distance
Of my dreams,
I see the colour
Of tomorrow.
In the horizon
Of my life,
I hear the calls
Of my sorrow.

Stacy Akers, Bishop Auckland, County Durham

WRITER'S BLOCK

I pick up my pen
And attempt to write,
But nothing comes
So I turn off the light.

Morning comes
I try again,
Still nothing there
Stupid brain!

I sit and think
Think and sit,
Still nothing comes,
I think I'll quit!

Christine Robinson, Peterlee, County Durham

GREEN FINGERS ON A DARK DAY

My willow is sad today
and clouds come to blanket
the sky, like a shroud.
The water is dark, unrippled.

No green-winged fowl to glide gracefully,
dipping and ducking
and making me laugh.

My willow weeps alone; green fingers trail
the water. Torrents of rain bow her low.
The park is deserted and the sand-coloured
walls of the castle are drenched by storm.

Only I, soaked and beaten by the elements,
walk around the lake; burdened
by a heavy heart,
I weep with my willow.

Sara Newby, Darlington, County Durham

THE LOTTERY

If you're threescore and ten
... or thereabout
And you've got all your teeth
... or more or less,
Your eyes still scan pictures
TV and books,
You've still got a figure
And some of your looks,
You still grace the dancefloor
And enjoy to the end -
You don't need the lottery
You've won it my friend!

Sheila Stephenson, South Sheilds, Tyne & Wear

THE GREAT PERPETRATOR

Set in my own octoplasm where
time is timeless and space endless.
Luminous body, medial of revolving earth:

reviver of life or life's death.
Superior to my cold counterpart ...
no thing or being am I ...
Without fear or controversy
I control all and everything.
Idol for worshippers - healer,
killer with power to perpetrate arson.
No one dare touch - fingers point
but eyes cannot mirror my glare
yet I can hide behind "acts of God"?
alternately set in my ways - rising
to no one but above and beyond everyone,
I am the "energy force" of all life
animal, vegetable and mineral.
If I cease to be so shall all.
Who am I?

Isabella F Veitch, Berwick-upon-Tweed, Northumberland

ANATOMY

A car has an engine pieced together by man
Man can take it to bits, put it back together again
He can add to it, take away from it
The same is of the human mind
The human body has an engine
Just like in a car
The brain motivates the body
Moves the limbs as it were
Who else could put together this human body of ours
How could the human body do the things it were capable of
If it weren't for the spiritual power of our everlasting God
Some say we evolved from the big big bang! But even so
Without the divine power who would we be?
Animals, plants, the beauty of a flower
Look closely at the way they grow!
Some of us doubt God's presence why?
Because we don't see him it must be a lie

We can't see the light that comes from electricity
Nor can we see the wind that flows through the trees

> *Pauline Thompson, Gateshead, Tyne & Wear*

NOTHING WITHOUT YOU

Anything beautiful or good inside of me
Is all for you.
Whether I grow rich, famous, successful, old,
It is all for you.
Everything I do, it's all for you.
To be worthy of you,
For you to look on me with pride.
When you love me I love myself,
When you don't want me I'm worthless.
You are my reason for breathing.
I will prove myself to you
And make you smile.
I love you;
You are my soul-mate.

> *James McLeish, Washington, Tyne & Wear*

LIFE

Young creature, stand up.
Now your first breath is taken
It's now time to live.

Strange people, strange house.
Did you know they existed?
It's now time to learn

Old child, adult life.
You're growing up so quickly.
It's now time to love

Enter the church doors
Greet your love from down the aisle.
It's time to protect.

Giving birth, new life,
A tribute, a dawning day.
It's time to move on.

Entering old age,
You've lived your life as you want
It's time to give up.

Louise Shepherd, Newcastle, Tyne & Wear

HEAVEN HELP

I've called on the spirits,
To untwist my mind,
And to all of my questions,
The answers to find.

I've called on the angels,
Please bring my heart peace,
From a tortuous love,
Which refuses to cease.

I've called on Lord Jesus,
Come lay on your hands,
To vanquish my demons,
And their dark demands.

I've called to my Father,
In heaven by prayer,
Release me from life,
And bitter despair.

Lucy McCollin, Hull, East Yorkshire

BUT STILL ...

The house in my eightieth year,
Creaks,
But I care not,
It will see me out, no doubt.
The windows grow dim,
Long before twilight.
But I clean them not,
Are not my eyes dim also?

Housebound,
No longer house proud,
I rattle like a nut in my dusty shell
But still,
The birds sing as sweetly
In my garden of weeds,

As they ever did ...

     Bill Elder, Bridlington, East Yorkshire

AFRICA CALLING

Here am I, blooming like a crimson, damask rose,
My roots set firm in English soil.
Here they are, my precious, copper children,
shining-eyed;
Learning, growing, marking time.
Far away he waits, my husband, youthful still,
For our return.
Life is good; I do not care to leave
My friends, my home, this independent life,
But Africa is calling.
In dreams I see that once familiar land.
In vain I strive to push it all away,
To sweep it under the new lounge carpet,
For beyond the pastel shades of Springtime

Lies his gleaming, hunter's form,
Dark beneath the moon;
Shining ...
Twining ...
To make me one with him again.

Jean Oxley, Scarborough, North Yorkshire

MID-LIFE BLUES

I've reached a certain age you know, have I really passed my prime?
My boobs are heading southwards, it's such a bloody crime.
My skin's gone slack around the jowls, no chiselled cheek-bones now.
The chasmed crowsfeet wrinkles, moisturising now a vow.

I've spent mounds of cash on miracles, believed advertising lies.
How could I be so gullible, goes to show hope never dies.
My confidence is shattered, frowning makes the wrinkles worse.
I am on a downward spiral, that can never be reversed.

I never was a glamour puss, more like an ungroomed tabby,
but it really hurts your ego when your body goes all flabby.
I still look good in candlelight and a girdle fools the eye.
More Wonderbras, God bless them, are all I need to buy.

So take me somewhere dimly lit and waltz me round the floor.
Life could be worse, it's only age.
A number, nothing more!

Patricia Pearson, Selby, North Yorkshire

REAL FEARS

There are crocodiles under my bed.
If I keep my hands under the covers, they can't get me.
The dressing gown hung from a hook, with its heavy collar,
Is an executioner, biding his time.

Oh no! The cupboard is open.
The witch is going to come out,
With her green skin, red eyes and pointed fingers,
And get me.

Dad's an alcoholic and mum's a nervous wreck,
But tonight, what's really got me worried
Is the bug-eyed purple spotted monster, coming through the window
To eat me.

    Candice Jones, Northallerton, North Yorkshire

THE WRITE STUFF

He scatters them haphazardly
Around his house: Grisham's latest hardback,
By the recliner say; or the collected poems
Of Sylvia Plath, wedged ever so invitingly
Between Delia and a toast rack,
Just above the aga range.

Meanwhile the TLS can be spotted,
By a seasoned observer, in the greenhouse,
Keeping his dahlias above freezing.
Be on the lookout also, for an Exchange & Mart,
Probably under the cellular phone in the conservatory.
And it's a pound to a penny
that The Star will be within easy reach
In the outside kazi,
Particularly on the occasion of a full moon.

He's so clever
And he wants people to know it.
He needs to show them you see,
That he is passionately interested in reading.

                              Alan Glasby, York, North Yorkshire

MEMORIES

Dead soldiers lap the unforgiving shores
Somewhere in heaven they're opening doors
The souls of the broken litter the land
These are the doves that fly to God's hand

Perhaps in the morning the sun will shine
We might understand in the fullness of time
Love can build bridges that fire can't cross
But filthy stains of the war will never wash

Sights of the battle burn deep in the eyes
Old seasoned troops, are brave yet wise
Moving in circles in the old campaign
Nothing is fresh but the stinging rain

Should they push on when they can't even see?
If the whole rank is wiped out who's there to please?
No fearing the bullet that bears their name
Killing is pointless and against the grain

                    Michael Bramley, Skipton, North Yorkshire

THE DRAGONFLY

Over the green weed-waving pools
Where creeping currents come to rest,
A lustrous dart of diverse hues
Manoeuvres deftly in its quest.

Descendant of an ancient line
It hovers, gauzy wings spread wide,
Entraps its prey then speeds away
To cruise the teeming waterside.

In shady dens of clustered stems
This rainbowed form, of dazzling skill,
Glows rich as stained glass in a church,
Then leaves - reversing - gleaming still.

The hunt resumes for insects small
By willows softly whispering;
Though of short life, this jewel bright
Lives on in nymphs, its own offspring.

June Long, Thirsk, North Yorkshire

WENSLEYDALE

Summer sun brings into life
That may began
To sleep on undulating lays
To give a domino pattern
Among swathes of green
A bleating sound to mothers call
An echo to the hills
Roving is its daily pleasure
With a melancholy stare

George Burgin, Rotherham, South Yorkshire

PISTOLS AT DAWN

Towing a backdrop of stark light dawning,
the curtains of darkness open the morning,
revealing the scene of a timeless test,
two generals who duel for title of best.

With pounding artillery paving their way,
ten thousand trained soldiers into the fray,
bravely they charged, screaming they fell,
fuelling the fire in the furnace of hell.

Draining dreams dripped for a sea of mud,
hungrily feasting from the platter of blood,
each dream dreamed of the dream's battle won,
some dreams lost with the dead tally done.

The winner stood up and proposed a toast,
"To me the victor, I've killed the most,"
Gracefully his opponent concedes defeat,
"To you the champion, I'm soundly beat."

                              Glenn Granter, Barnsley, South Yorkshire

TOYBOYS

I need some sex
I said, flicking through the yellow pages
between religion, security, shopping centres and slimming products,
finding none.

And love?
There between locks and mortgages,
loft conversions, luggage and maternity wear
drew another blank.

The hunt for men led to
meat - wholesale,
minibuses, mirrors and mobile phones,
tempting only with medical waste.

And so to boys.
Boys revealed bouncing castles and inflatables hire.
Let your fingers do the walking.

Beats making that call.

        Rebecca Wolman, Sheffield, South Yorkshire

HOME

I walked along the waterside
the breeze was blowing light
in the twilight of the evening
before it turns to night
I look towards the hills beyond
and memories of you
come to my mind as easy
as the sunlight passing through
I think of precious times gone by
spent looking at this scene.
On the water and the hills and glens
so peacefully serene
I hope that you remember
and a picture springs to mind
to bring you happy memories of
the love you left behind.

Christina Anderson, Inverness, Invernesshire

NOTHING COMES CLOSE TO COOL BLACK TARMAC

You laughed at first at my
Too cripple, too high, high-heels.
You shouted at last when I put
naked hot feet on deep heavy road.
I felt such release and relief;
the contact of strong wet stone
with my blistering toes.

You were afraid of glass and stones
like arguments simple and small can
cut deep and hard and painful.
As I walk along my road
I'm aware of the danger and the pain.
But to stand still is agony

I'll smile and skip over the stones.

Here, I'll help you take off your shoes,
Drunken laughter and socks on the night pavement.
We'll walk together, naked feet
to avoid the glass and stones,
following the path down our road.
stumbling laughter and skin slapping on tarmac
Twenty toes against the world.

Shona Ritch, Orkney, Orkney Isles

DESERT SONG

Behold here these desert sands,
all golden dust; this sun's anvil
burning under eternal noontides

Parched and dewless,
this shifting wind-blown mantle
was never still nor conquered

Dunes sombre under night's dark dome
are struck with blazing swordlight,
are illumined by ancient stars

Mount seven dunes, sail seven oases
Ford unnumbered dust-dry rivers
Come, weeping, back
for thirst.

Gillian Robin, Strathaven, South Lanarkshire

SEEDS OF SATISFACTION

I look upon the fruits of my womb and know that I did well
My flesh, my blood, my tears and pain, I would do it all again

My son, my babe, a boy, a man, a caring person since his life began
Tall and handsome he stands out in a crowd, I've watched him grow and I feel proud
My daughter, my babe, a girl - A woman, pretty, bright
And so unassuming
Strong yet fragile she is always my friend, of her father and I a delicate blend.
When my life seems to hold no great attraction,
I look at them both the seeds of my satisfaction.

Marie Hunter, Edinburgh, West Lothian

SEA HORSES

Out of the tumbling waves they came
With threshing tail and flowing mane,
So lovely in the dying sun,
Their movement made me want to run
To join them in their graceful play,
To live my life their carefree way.

I watched with envy while they ran
Across the shining, silver sand,
Their every limb was stretched with ease,
In perfect rhythm with the breeze.
The wind obeyed their every call,
I wished I could be with them all.

They frolicked in the cool sea air,
Prancing on without a care.
I saw the dancing waves at play,
And they alone all seemed to say,
Your hour has passed, the day is done,
And they returned whence they had come.

Sheila Ann Munro, Dundee, Tayside

STRAGGLERS OF AUTUMN

end of summer sloughs a frosty sigh
which skitters the roses into contrition
bequeathing them the muse of stillness
within that tinted epoch vein
that is the weeping seed
of dazed days to rise and come
days that bear the knitted sheen of autumn

a lake which once knew rowdy ripples
now knows only a smirking sky
into which picnic laughter floats
to drown in the snobbish depths
where crowds of lost angels giggle
fugitives of hard times and sour tides
whose pleasure is to mock the stragglers of autumn

Albert Gamage, Irvine, North Ayrshire

WINTER CREEPS

Winter creeps, its evil spell
Killing, destroying and raping
The majesty of Spring.

Autumn, the world grows old
It gives up its best
And withers up the worst.

Summer, forgotten so rapidly
A time of sun, warmth, joy,
Obliterated by the cold chill of dawn.

Spring, where are you? time of rebirth,
time of renewal, entrenched in stillness
the cold, hard earth, yields to small rays

Glimmer of hope, the Spring of my life.
Fertility of Summer, joy. Lost,
In the Autumn of my heart,
Before the death of Winter.

                Cate Campbell, Aberdeen, Aberdeenshire

BLEACHED BONES

Great barren ravine
Rocky outcrop
Hot sun beating down
No food, no water

Man there all alone
Lonely, weary
Searching for shade
Sweltering in heat
Desperate
Crawls to cave

Then; a sound
Long guttural growl
Sun glinting off sharp, red eyes
Bleached bones on hot sands

                Tim West, Stonehaven, Aberdeenshire

FEAR STALKS OUR STREETS

In bygone days
In the Scotland of my youth
Fear in city streets
Was unknown.
But today?
In our glorious new Millennium?
To walk in the darkness
To the post-box ...

That is an expedition
Fraught with raw fear ...
A journey into the unknown.

                    Jenny Chaplin, Largs, Ayrshire

INSIDE

Sleep inside me
Tonight.
Slow moving
Breaths.
Quietly touching
Bones.
Warm hands
Resting.
Evening kisses
Drifting.
The moon,
Blessing our souls
As you lie,
Tonight,
Inside me,
Sleeping.

              Michelle Melville, Fort William, Inverness-shire

YESTERDAY

Yesterday with a whole afternoon off
I went to buy a birthday card in town
Something that would give the boy a laugh
Life was hard, with his big exams up soon.
I went through busy streets and shopping malls
And saw old men, retired or redundant,
Talking to cronies, leaning against walls,
Shopping with the wife, non communicant.
In their eyes was a sort of vacancy;

Far removed from the bustle of the street,
That dreamt of days of work and dignity
When time to shop, like this, seemed quite a treat.

When I am superannuated soon
I'll not go shopping in the afternoon.

Andrew Burnside, Falkirk, Stirlingshire

PABLO

I knew Picasso when the memory of Guernica
still ravaged his mind with a picture of -
frightened fleeing horses heedless of the
children on the ground, the frenzied prayers
to a God who seemed too far, and men
screaming in the fire of their frustration
because they could not reach the sky.

It was not a good time, for the agony
had not been laid to rest as it rests now
on the sale-room wall.

His moment of joy and pain has passed,
those restless hands are now forever still.

The gallery will open after lunch and
'experts' who never saw the colours that
lay beyond his eyes, or felt a wound
will come to sit in judgement of his scars.

Jack Pollock, Glasgow, Strathclyde